Defensive End

Learning More about Anxiety and
Communication with Help from
Gramps

James Shaw

**This book may be ordered by contacting
James Shaw, PsyD, at www.drjshaw.com.**

Because of the dynamic nature of the Internet, any Web
addresses or links contained in this book may have changed
since publication and may no longer be valid.

ISBN: 1495968790, ISBN-13: 978-1495968792

Printed in the United States of America

Disclaimer: The information, ideas and suggestions in this
book are not intended as a substitute for professional advice.
Before following any suggestions contained in this book, you
should consult your personal physician or mental health
professional. The author shall not be liable or responsible for
any loss or damage allegedly arising as a consequence of your
use of application of any information or suggestions in this
book.

Author's note: This book is a work of fiction, with the
exception of historical facts and locations. Names, characters
and incidents are the product of the author's imagination or
are used fictitiously. Any resemblance to actual events or
persons, living or dead, is coincidental.

To my son, Randy,
whom I watched score touchdowns and play
defense as a young football player and who has
grown into a successful businessman and family
man.

Contents

—✦—

Batting Third 1

Opportunity 9

Rocky Times.. 17

Awful Accident.. 25

Hungarian Family.. 33

A Slight Edge... 43

Breaking the Law 55

History Lesson 65

Madamoiselle 75

Pushing Buttons... 83

Second Half.. 93

Hot Chow 103

Get Out... 113

Weighing-In 123

Rivalry Game..133

School Dance...145

Basketball Tryouts 153

Giving Thanks 163

Truthful End 171

Batting Third

I t was Saturday, June 20, 1970. My team was playing our last game of the Bronco League baseball season. This was my third straight year being on the Cardinals with my best friend, Stan. It was the top half of the fifth inning. There were two out and no one on base with Stan up to bat. Stan was the number two hitter in the lineup as he had been since I'd started playing with him. But now I was on deck. I'd always wanted to be the number three hitter and was so excited that I'd finally been given this spot for every game this year. Third was a thrill because this was the first year I'd batted any higher than sixth in a lineup. Stan took the count to 2-2 before getting a solid base hit to right field.

Stan was a very patient hitter. He would take a lot of pitches until he got the one he wanted to hit. I, on the other hand, had always been an aggressive hitter, trying to hit the first good pitch for two reasons: First, for every strike I let go by without swinging, it gave me less swings to try to get a base hit. Second, for every pitch I took, I had a better chance of getting hit by the pitch. I didn't fear getting hit by the pitch now like I once did, but I still didn't particularly like it. Even getting a walk was one less chance at hitting a homerun. Most

1

baseball experts would agree that the patient approach is better, but I found what worked for me.

I had to make one compromise in my approach while hitting third in the lineup, because often Stan, a good base stealer, was on first and wanted to steal second on the first pitch. Stan almost always let the first pitch go by without swinging if there was a runner on first base to allow him to steal. So the compromise was that I would take the first pitch, unless the pitch was over the center of the plate and I thought I could it hit hard and drive it to the outfield. I probably took the first pitch about two-thirds of the time with a runner on first, even though I can't remember seeing too many pitches I didn't like. If I put the ball in play on the first pitch, Stan had a running start, similar to a hit-and-run play. In the Bronco League we were able to lead off. This was a big advantage for stealing bases, but we had to be aware of being picked off.

I walked up to the plate as I looked down at Stan on first base. He started running as the pitcher delivered a fat pitch right over the inside part of the plate about belt high. I swung and hit the ball hard and in the air down the third base line. I immediately started running as fast as I could. At the Clifford H. Smart Junior High School baseball fields, there were no outfield fences, so there were no over-the-wall homeruns. All homeruns had to be *legged out*. As I rounded first, I saw the leftfielder chasing after the ball, and I knew I had a chance for a homerun. I rounded second at full speed and could see the third base coach waving me home. As I rounded third, I had my back to the relay throw, so I just kept running hard and stepped on home plate well before the throw. It was my third homerun of the year! Well, this was my third true homerun, because I actually got all the way home five times. But the other two were bad throws to third base as I was arriving there, and I was able to go home after the overthrow. I have matured in my official scoring. Two years ago, these would have been homeruns in my book, but now they count as triples and making it home on the error. That homerun made the score 9-3, with us on top.

The other players started congratulating me as soon as I crossed the plate. I was happy, but I played it cool as I had before. I didn't get too excited, and I hoped people would see that this was the way I expected to hit every time. I heard a monologue from a Bill Cosby album where he said he usually didn't celebrate his sports successes for the same reason. However, I had started playing it cool two years before Cosby released his album.

Two years ago, in the Mustang League, I was so happy to play almost every inning at first base. When I got to the Bronco League last year and played with Marty, who threw left handed, it only made sense that he played first base when he didn't pitch. So I was given the opportunity to learn several new positions last year. I played second base, as well as outfield, and I still played first base while Marty was pitching. Last year Marty's father was the head coach and Stan's father the assistant coach. Marty was in our grade at school, but he was a year older, so I only played every other year with him. Last year, since I was one of the younger boys at 11 years old in a league of 11- and 12-year-olds, I was happy that I played an important role on the team. I ended up hitting .350 with three doubles and 16 stolen bases. I didn't have any triples or homeruns.

I continued to play the neighborhood games, which helped my game a lot. Stan and I also went to a week-long baseball camp the summer after my first year of Bronco League that helped me develop hitting skills. The coaches at the camp showed me how to improve my stance and swing. They helped me hit balls in all areas of the strike zone and tried to help me to "lay off" pitches outside the strike zone. I learned to notice whether the pitcher was throwing a fastball, change up or curve, so I could get ready to hit whatever kind of pitch was thrown. To get the money to go to the camp, I had a paper route for about 5 months last year.

In the bottom of the fifth inning, I took my position at first base. In the Bronco League, pitchers were allowed to pitch 10 innings a week and we played four games a week if there were no rainouts. We had two pitchers who would each start two games a week and try to go five innings each game. If it wasn't going well, our catcher would pitch a little too. Stan pitched the sixth and seventh innings, the final innings, of every game, plus extra innings, if needed. In the bottom of the sixth inning, when Stan would pitch, Coach put me at shortstop. It was a great way for me to get to learn the shortstop position.

In this sixth inning, the other team's first batter hit a hard ground ball up the middle that Stan, on the pitcher's mound, barely touched with his glove. I was at shortstop and, seeing the ball go up the middle, I headed to my left. But when Stan deflected the ball, I had to stop and go back to my right. I fielded the ball, but it was too late to throw to first to get the runner out.

On the first pitch to the next batter, the runner at first tried to steal second. Our second baseman covered the bag, but the throw from the catcher was in the dirt and got by him. Luckily, I had hustled over to back up the play, and I stopped the ball so the runner couldn't advance.

Stan and I had worked on a pickoff play with our second baseman, and this was the last game of the season, so we decided to try it. The second baseman faked like he was going to go to second base and then went back to his position. I sprinted to second base. Stan twirled and threw the ball to me, but the runner had started running to third. I took a step toward the outfield so my throw to third wouldn't hit the runner in the back and made a good throw to our third baseman, who got his glove in a position to tag the runner. It appeared he was out. Our play had worked! Then I heard the umpire say, "Safe!"

At this point, I had been practicing my anger-control techniques for years and had played enough baseball to know the umpire is human and makes mistakes. I quickly assessed the situation. Was this umpire's decision going to cost us the game? No. I quickly said to myself that we were up by six runs. This run didn't really matter, and it was nothing to get angry about. I turned and looked at Stan. We both shook our heads and smiled at one another.

In the top of the seventh inning, Stan hit a double. I would now get to bat and maybe hit my second homerun of the game. What a way to end the season! Since Stan was already on second base, I wouldn't have to watch any pitches. I wanted my last at bat to be special.

"Tom, come on back to the bench. Tim is going to pinch hit for you."

I was stunned as I walked back to the bench—and very disappointed.

As I got back to the bench, Coach came up to me. "Tom, I know you love to hit, but we've got this game in hand. I want Tim to get a chance to bat."

"Coach, I know. I just really wanted to make my last at bat of the season a great one."

"Two years ago, your last at bat of the season was a very memorable homerun. You'll always get to remember that your last at bat of this season was a homerun too."

"You're right, Coach," I said softly, still feeling sad. "Tim needs to make a memory for his last at bat of the season. I had mine two innings ago."

Tim had had a tough season and hadn't gotten that many hits. This time he was able to get a solid base hit, and I could see him smiling at first base. I still had some work to do to overcome my selfishness, but I was trying my best. Seeing how happy Tim was really helped me to overcome my feelings. And, we won our last game of the season.

Our team did very well. We were 18 wins and only 10 losses. I'd kept track of my statistics like I'd done the previous two years: I batted .624

(68 for 109) with 12 doubles, 4 triples, and 3 homeruns. I also had 54 RBIs, scored 41 runs, and stole 31 bases. I didn't know what Stan's stats were, but he seemed to put up similar numbers to mine. We were the one-two punch in the lineup, and the season had been very enjoyable.

Later that evening, my mother and I went to visit her parents, Grandma and Grandpa Mochina, in the city. When we arrived, Grandpa was complaining about the Tigers.

"They can't hit. It's really bad when you lose 2-1 and your only run is a homerun by your pitcher!" Grandpa exclaimed. "They're getting too old and can't hit. We should not lose to the Indians."

He was referring to pitcher Earl Wilson, who had homered for the only run. The Tigers had a winning percentage hovering around .500 and weren't in first place this year.

Stan was excited about the Tigers this year because they had a young Polish shortstop named Ken Szotkiewicz. He hit left-handed and threw right-handed like Stan. I knew of one Hungarian players in the major leagues: Al Hrabosky of the St. Louis Cardinals. I wouldn't have known his heritage except that he went by the nickname of the *Mad Hungarian*. I was happy that he came into the league after I already had the established nickname of *The Machine* or this might have become my nickname too.

Sometimes when we went to my grandparents on a Saturday evening, my mother had a date planned. But she didn't have a date on this particular night. My mother still had another month before her thirty-first birthday. She was tall for a lady with blond hair and blue eyes and looked like she could be an actress. I never understood why she dated men who were nowhere close to being in her league. But she did not seem to appreciate me telling her this after every man she met.

After dinner, we played the card game euchre. My mother was my partner, and my grandparents were our opponents. We all had quick minds and the ability to keep track of almost every card played. I had fun playing, and it was easy to see where I got my intelligence from.

"You can't always get what you want.
You can't always get what you want.
But if you try sometimes well you might find,
You get what you what you need."
— *The Rolling Stones (1969)*

Opportunity

A t the end of the season, the coaches selected five players from each team to try out for a traveling all-star team. There were six teams, so 30 players got to try out. Stan and I were two of the players from our team who were picked to try out. We did really well in the two practices and felt that we should make the team. After the second practice, the head coach, who was the coach of the first-place team in our league, announced that we would get a call to let us know which 15 players had made the team, and which 15 did not. During the practices I hit well and shared first-base duties with two others. Stan shared the shortstop duties with three others.

After that second practice, Stan and I agreed to call each other after we got our calls. I went home and waited and finally got the call that I had made the city all-star team. I called Stan, and he had made the team too! We had our first game coming up. It would be played as the first game of a two-game knockout, tournament style. We had to come in at least in second place to advance to the next weekend of all-stars.

I arrived at the first all-star game and couldn't wait to see where I would bat in the lineup and what position I would play. I was very disappointed to find I was not even starting the game. Worse yet, I did not even play in the first game. Stan batted ninth and played centerfield. We were the only two players from our team to be on this all-star team. We lost the first game 8-3.

I went home very unhappy. Why did I not get to play? Would I get to play in the second game? If we lost the second game, it would be over.

For the second game, I arrived at the park and warmed up. I couldn't wait for the lineup to be announced. Except for the starting pitcher, the lineup was the same, so it didn't include me. I was again disappointed and had a hard time staying "up" for the game. I'm sure it showed on my face.

We were down 6-2 in the sixth inning when the coach called on me to pinch hit for our first baseman. He had struck out in his first two plate appearances. On the third pitch, I lined a ball to right for a base hit. The coach had asked me not to try to steal when we were down four runs, so I stayed at first. The hitter after me struck out, and I didn't get to advance. After that I went in to play first base for one inning, but we lost the game and my brief Bronco League all-star career came to an end. I was disappointed about my playing time, but I was happy that I did well when given a chance. The coach came up to me after the game and said that he'd kept me on the team because I was one of the best pure hitters he'd ever seen in the Bronco League. I thanked him, but I didn't understand why he would say this and not play me.

I heard my mother talking on the phone after my two all-star games. She was telling someone that I only got to bat once because I didn't have a father and all of the boys who played had fathers watching them. At first I dismissed this thought as ridiculous. What would having a father have to do with me not playing? Then my thoughts turned to the starting first baseman, who'd struck out in most of his at bats. His father was a prominent business owner in town. Was that how he got the start over me?

After thinking for a while, I got my bathing suit on and walked down to the lake. I saw Gramps out practicing horseshoes, so I went over and talked to him.

Gramps was my neighbor who lived on the lake a short walk from my house. I think he had asked me to call him Gramps instead of Dr. Davis as a way to make our relationship more informal. His grandchildren called him Gramps as well. He didn't seem that old to me, so Gramps seemed like a funny name for him. Our ages were 50 years apart but he had a way of making me laugh and helping me in a subtle way.

Gramps and I had developed a strong bond years ago, and I found him to be a very wise teacher. He would ask me questions in such a way that really helped me understand what he was teaching me. He told me jokes, let me swim at his beach, let me take his row boats on the lake, and played horseshoes with me, but most of all he talked to me and gave me ideas about how to meet my goals.

When I was having a lot of trouble in school and fighting anyone who did anything I didn't like, Gramps taught me techniques for controlling my anger. When I avoided activities that were important to meet my goals, such as talking to girls, Gramps would help me by telling me it was okay to feel uncomfortable if that helped me focus on my goals. Most of all, Gramps taught me that I could recover from embarrassing mistakes.

"Hey, Gramps."

"Tom, how are you? Any homeruns today?"

"No, the all-stars are over. It was a two-game knockout, and we lost the first two games. I only got one at bat and got a base hit. I really want to play on the Detroit Tigers one day, and I can't even start for some local 12-year-olds all-star team."

"It sounds like you could have started for the team, but this particular coach didn't choose you. It's too bad there isn't a game three because after getting a hit today, he might have asked you to start tomorrow."

"Maybe," I said, still frowning.

"Tom, no matter how hard we try in life, we can't always determine our fate. Sometimes we need someone to take a chance on us. For every major league baseball player, there are at least three other guys with just as much talent who no one took a chance on."

"Why?"

"There are a number of reasons. There are very few major leaguers who are labeled as *can't miss*. For most players, there's someone who takes a chance on them, not knowing if they'll be good enough. If you get that chance, it's up to you what you do with it."

"I don't get any chances."

"Tom, you had a much better chance than many other boys. You signed up for baseball and your coach took a chance on you to be the number three hitter in the order. Did you show him he made a good decision or a bad decision?"

"I was determined to show him he made a great decision, and I had an outstanding season."

"Your coach took a chance on you. Then 30 guys tried out for an all-star team, and that coach only gave the opportunity to half those players. He took a chance on you. You worked hard and put yourself in a good position to be an all-star starter. Can you still be a Detroit Tiger?"

"I'm not sure."

"I'm not sure either, but if you quit playing baseball now, I'll be sure you won't make it. You have to keep on playing and maybe someday someone will take a chance on you to join the Detroit Tigers."

"Why didn't you play for the Tigers?"

"Tom, I wanted to play very badly. But after hitting .500 my senior year of high school and playing well at third base, no major league team offered me a chance. I really wanted to keep playing, so I looked into college ball, but no major college was willing to take a chance on me."

"So what did you do?"

"There was a baseball coach at Alma, nicknamed the Colonel, who wanted to take a chance on me."

"*Elma*? The only *Elma* I know is Elmer Fudd from Bugs Bunny."

Gramps laughed. "There's a small private college in central Michigan called Alma—A-L-M-A—College, and I went there to play baseball and get an education. The coach at Alma took a chance on me, and I had a great experience. Realizing I wasn't going to get an opportunity to play baseball after college, I decided to try medical school. I applied to ten schools, including Michigan, Pitt,

Case Western Reserve, Ohio State, and Penn State, but all of them turned me down."

"Turned YOU down? I can't believe it."

"Yes, but one school, Michigan State University, took a chance on me, not knowing for certain if I would be a good doctor. It only took one school. If I would've been selected by all of those schools, I could only go to one anyway. I was lucky. If State wouldn't have taken a chance on me, my life might have been different. I would've found something else. In life, we get a lot of rejections, but we have to keep trying until someone takes a chance on us. And when they do, we have to make the most of it. Our job is to put ourselves in the best position to get someone to take a chance on us."

I knew Gramps was telling me to keep trying. I just never thought that some of the Detroit Tigers had been rejected until someone took a chance on them. Gramps has been a top doctor for a lot of years, but back when he was younger, he needed someone to take a chance on him. After that day I always remembered this, and knew I had to put myself in a position for someone to take a chance on me.

On Tuesday, I had agreed to meet Stan at his beach, so I went down to the lake to borrow a row boat from Gramps. Sure, I could swim at Gramps' beach, but I would be swimming alone. There was much more going on down at Stan's neighborhood beach. Gramps had a notebook in the boat house, and if I took a boat out when he wasn't there, he just asked that I wrote a note in the notebook saying when I took the boat and what time I would bring it back. I was very good about getting the boat back on time. I wore a waterproof watch that I'd gotten with my birthday money so I always knew the time.

The last two summers, I had to spend four days each week at my grandparents' house. But I spent Wednesdays at Gramps' lake house helping him with chores in the mornings. This year I'd pestered my mother, telling her that since I was an adult now (at 12 years of age), I should be able to stay home by myself during the summer. My mother agreed to this but told me if I got into trouble I would have to return to going to the city four days a week with my grandparents.

This summer I still helped Gramps every Wednesday morning. Other days I stayed home to watch TV, read, draw, listen to music or play one of my games. Several days throughout the week, I would row a boat down to Stan's neighborhood beach. We would play catch, Frisbee or just talk and soak up the rays.

I arrived at Stan's beach and pulled my boat up on shore. Stan had his beach blanket in a prime spot so we could people watch.

"Tom, you row that boat like a machine! You're getting as strong as an ox! How am I going to keep up with you?" said Stan with a smile as I approached.

We had fun teasing each other with the nicknames the parents on our baseball teams had given us. We were now called these nicknames in baseball, football and basketball. Stan was called *The Man* after Stan Musial. I was called *The Machine*, which was my last name without the last syllable.

"My goal is to keep up with The Man, but I've been thinking I'm ready for that two spot in the lineup," I told him. We both laughed.

We didn't really talk about the all-star game. We just laughed and had a good time. Then Ed, who was a year older than us, walked up. I knew him from playing in the neighborhood games.

"Hey, how are you two hippies today?"

"Hippies? You have longer hair than either one of us, and I think that Speedo qualifies you as a hippie," replied Stan.

"Hey, this Speedo is cool. The girls like it."

We all laughed.

"I was talking to Rocky and Danny, and they wonder why you guys don't ever talk to them," Ed reported.

"Rocky and Danny? I've never heard of those guys. Who are they?" I asked.

Ed laughed. "I don't think they're too happy with you two. They're starting to think you guys are stuck up and won't talk to people."

"How come I don't know them?" asked Stan.

"They're going into the ninth grade. Since they live on the north side of the lake, they go to West Bloomfield schools. If I see them out today, I'll come and get you guys to introduce you."

I wondered about these two guys. Why would two ninth graders from West Bloomfield schools want to meet us? I wondered if they wanted to fight us or try to bully us in some way. Lucky for Stan and me, the potential bullies didn't show up that day.

"I'll take your part when darkness comes,
And pain is all around.
Like a bridge over troubled water, I will lay me down.
Like a bridge over troubled water, I will lay me down."
— *Simon & Garfunkel (1969)*

Rocky Times

"Tom! Let's go!" my mother cried firmly. I walked out of my bedroom looking down. "I'm ready," I said. "Okay, let's get in the car. We have to leave."

Over the past several years, when it had come time to go to the dentist, I flat out refused. I just found it terrifying to sit in the dentist's chair while they scraped my teeth. I felt like one slip and the dentist would stab me. I threw such a fuss about this that my mother would finally give in and let me miss the appointment. Lately, some of my teeth had been aching.

—◆—

A month ago, my mother had urged me to talk to Gramps about going to the dentist, so I did. Gramps told me he didn't like going to the dentist either, but he went every seven months. He would tell the people at the dental office how busy his schedule was so that he could stretch out the appointments from every six months to seven months.

Gramps smiled as he told me this, and I could see he found a victory in doing something he didn't like. He told me he went because he wanted to avoid that really bad dental work like dentures, crowns and fillings. When he said dentures, I thought about Grandma and Grandpa Mochina constantly taking their false teeth out because they hurt them. I found this really gross. Gramps told me he still had his teeth, but had several cavities and some crowns.

Gramps convinced me that I should go to the dentist to avoid dentures and get my cavities fixed. I told Gramps I just couldn't imagine sitting there with my mouth open and letting someone hurt me. Gramps reminded me that if my goal was to have teeth, I should give up one hour of my life and endure the pain and discomfort. He told me the people at the dental office would try their best not to inflict pain, but it could be painful, and it was my job to sit in the chair and not let them see that I was afraid.

The conversation continued, and I reminded Gramps that he had once given me a one to ten scale of things I didn't like. Even though the dentist wasn't trying to kill me, he would be inflicting pain, and this seemed like an eight or nine on the scale. Gramps told me some medical and dental procedures were painful, and I would have to tolerate this pain for the goal of my health. He reminded me that the goal was to be healthy. Talking to him helped, and I decided that my goal would be to not make a scene at home or at the dental office because I was going to have to do this anyway, so I should make it the best experience I could.

— ◆ —

We drove to the dentist's office in my mother's year-old 1969 yellow Chevy Biscayne. She had finally had given up her Ford Falcon by selling it to her younger cousin, Rod. When we arrived at the dentist I wasn't the most talkative, but I did what I was told without fussing. When they called my name, my mother asked if I wanted her to go in with me, and I told her I would be okay by myself. As I sat in the chair with my head back and my mouth open, I endured the pain and said nothing. I did wince occasionally but did not make a sound. It was such a relief when the dentist told me I was all done. He told me to get my mother to meet him by the window. I assumed this was to settle the finances.

I went out to the lobby and told my mother how well I had done. My mother went up and talked to the dentist and then she told me it was time to go home. On the way home, she turned on the radio and we listened to some of the top hits of the day.

When we got home, my mother asked me to sit down because we needed to talk.

"Tom," she said as she closed her eyes for a few seconds, "you have to go back to another dentist in three weeks."

"What? Gramps told me that if I went in now, I wouldn't have to go back for seven months."

"That would have been the case, but you have some cavities. Five teeth need fillings and one..." She hesitated. "One needs to be extracted."

"Extracted? What do you mean?"

"Pulled. Removed."

I sat there trying to absorb what she'd said. "Will I need false teeth like Grandpa?"

"No, it will be a small gap that will eventually fill in."

"This sounds extremely painful. Much more painful than today."

"Yes, the dentist told me it would be so painful that he would need to have you put to sleep for the entire process."

"Put to sleep?" I said in a little louder voice. "I will not do that!"

"Tom, it will get really bad if you don't do it. Would you please talk to Gramps about it?"

"I'll talk to him, but I can't imagine he would want me to risk my life getting put to sleep and possibly never waking back up."

— ✦ —

From kindergarten through the fourth grade, I had a difficult time making friends. When I did make a friend, I found something to get mad about and destroyed the relationship. The last two years have gone much better mainly because of my relationship with Stan. Stan was popular, athletic and did well in school. I don't know what he liked about me, but he really seemed to enjoy my company. We laughed and talked a lot. We trusted each other. I didn't want to do anything to destroy that relationship. Stan and I have had some disagreements, but we both seem to value our friendship enough to work through any issues. I thought Mickey Dolenz was the best singer in The Monkees, Bill Freehan was the best Detroit Tiger, and "Signs" by the Five Man Electrical Band was the greatest song ever. Stan liked Davey Jones of The Monkees, Jim Northrup of the Tigers and thought "Joy to the World" by Three Dog Night was the greatest song ever. We kept a sense of humor about these disagreements.

We'd been in the same fifth-grade class, and we'd had a friendly competition to see who would get the best grades. Although Stan could run faster than me and had done better in sports, we found that I would usually get the better grades. There were times when Stan would get the higher grade, but I had certainly established myself as one of the top students.

We were put in separate classes in the sixth grade. We didn't like it at the time, but we were able to keep our special friendship and make friends with others as well. We would still get together at recess and on weekends. I was finally able to accept people as being different from me and not get angry at them. The work that I'd done with Gramps on not getting angry was very helpful in forming friendships.

In the fifth and sixth grades, there were no desk-flipping or chasing-someone-with-a-baseball-bat incidents. For the most part, I was able to keep calm using the thinking strategies Gramps had taught me. Every once in a while I would feel myself getting angry, but I would tell myself over and over that my goal was to not get into any trouble, and I was able to not react in these situations. We had a new principal at the start of fifth grade, and I am proud to say that I never stepped foot in his office. I'd known the previous principal all too well.

Saturday was the Fourth of July. In addition to the holiday, the excitement of the day was a new radio show hosted by Casey Kasem called America's Top 40. I listened from the number 40 song by Marvin Gaye through a bunch of hits at the time. Three of my favorite groups had songs that could be number one for the very first show: Three Dog Night, The Rolling Stones and The Jackson Five. The song "Mama Told Me Not to Come" by Three Dog Night was the first song to be number one in the countdown.

I couldn't help but think a little about the time I'd spent Independence Day with Teresa in the summer of 1968. I wondered when I would see her again since she went back to school in Livonia. I ended up seeing her three times during the summer of 1969. We talked briefly each time but the magic feeling was somehow lost. I hadn't seen her yet this summer. This year Gramps had invited my mother and me down to celebrate with his family.

On Sunday I called Stan and he agreed to meet me at the beach around 10:30 in the morning the next day. On Monday I got up and went down to Gramps' place to get a boat. I rowed over to Stan's beach, but as I approached the shore, I didn't see him, so I pulled the boat up, put my beach towel down, and waited.

"Tom! Good job, man! You claimed the prime spot. Help me get this big beach blanket down," said Stan when he walked up. Soon after, Ed also appeared.

"Hey, Rocky and Danny want you to put that blanket over by them so they can talk to you," said Ed.

"Where are they?" I asked.

"Come on. I'll take you over to them."

We followed Ed. When he stopped, we saw two older girls. Both were tanned and wearing bikinis. We'd certainly noticed these two before, but we figured they were high school girls.

"Rocky, Danny, meet The Man and The Machine," Ed said with a smile.

What? Rocky and Danny were beautiful girls? Why did they have these names? Talk about not what we expected...

"The Man and The Machine, hmmm," Rocky said with a big smile.

Rocky had bright blue eyes with curly blond hair. Danny was a straight-haired brunette with brown eyes. Both looked to be about 5' 8" and very slender.

"I'm Tom," I said, feeling embarrassed.

"I'm Stan," he said, seeming to shake.

I thought I was the anxious one, but as I looked at Stan, I could tell he was more nervous than I was. He might be very comfortable with sports, but being face-to-face with really good-looking girls seemed to put him out of his comfort zone.

"I've seen you guys here and was hoping you would come talk to us. Do you want to put your blanket down here?" said Rocky, gesturing to the spot next to hers.

We spread out our blanket. Rocky and I were next to each other. Stan was on the other side of me and Danny was on the other side of Rocky. Since I had lighter hair and Stan had darker hair, in our way of thinking, it only made sense that I would talk to Rocky. Rocky and I did most of the talking.

"So, I must admit, when I heard the name Rocky, you're not quite what I pictured," I told her.

Rocky started laughing. "I've heard that before. Danny and I live next door to one another. We like to play sports and be active more than we like to do girly things. Our real names are Roxanne and Danielle, but my dad called us Rocky and Danny. The names stuck, and they're now what we go by. Just like you and Stan are The Machine and The Man," Rocky said with a teasing smile.

I was stunned by how beautiful she was. To a boy going into seventh grade, she was a full-grown lady. That summer we had fun swimming and playing Frisbee. Even though she was two years older, we developed a really good relationship and looked forward to seeing each other. I really just enjoyed the time we spent together.

Stan and Danny played Frisbee and went swimming together but didn't talk as much as Rocky and I did. I finally saw a vulnerable side of the guy I really did consider to be *The Man*. I didn't realize he was shy around girls. I'd to work to get over my shyness with girls and I still had a long way to go, but I enjoyed Stan thinking that I was more comfortable talking to beautiful girls than he was.

"We're calling everyone to ride along,
To another shore,
We can laugh our lives away,
And be free once more."
— The Blues Image (1970)

Awful Accident

I really wanted to play quarterback this year on the football team. I had gotten a football for Christmas and when I didn't have anyone to throw with, I would go out in the snow and run around working on moves and balance. I used a tree to practice running the option play, pitching the ball and trying to hit the tree. I also practiced my passing using trees as my receivers.

I decided to bring my football with me in the boat to go to Stan's beach. When I got there, Stan and I threw the football back and forth as we each ran pass patterns. As we were throwing the football, Rocky and Danny walked up.

"How 'bout some two on two guys?" said Rocky, with her head playfully tilted to the side and a mischievous smile.

"Hey, Rocky. Hmmm, two on two?" I said as I started grinning.

"Yeah, two on two. Me and The Machine against the two of you," said Rocky, pointing to Danny and Stan.

Rocky and Danny were considerably taller than Stan and me. I was about 5' 3" and Stan was lucky to be 5' 1". I was one of the tallest 12-year-olds, but I was still much shorter than these 14-year-old 5' 8" ladies.

We had a lot of fun playing. My usual competitive nature never surfaced as I was mesmerized by these girls. Playing with Rocky, I learned to throw the ball so she could catch it. If I threw it too hard, she had a hard time. By floating the ball a little, I could make it so she could usually catch it.

After playing, Rocky asked if we could go for a ride in my row boat. I had considered the goal of taking a girl out in the row boat to be getting a kiss. Did Rocky want to kiss me? I wanted to kiss her, but it was still strange to me that she was so much older and taller. We ended up going for a fun ride, laughing and smiling most of the time. We had fun but she never acted like she wanted to kiss me.

—◆—

A few weeks later, the day arrived for my second dentist appointment. I knew I had to go, but I was not on my best behavior. I was scared when I got in the car with my mother and we drove to the appointment. As I sat in the waiting area, I could only think that I wanted to survive this day because I really wanted to see if I could play quarterback this football season.

I tried not to speak or squirm as I was lying on the operating table. They started an IV and then put a big brown block in my mouth that looked like the biggest piece of chocolate I had ever seen. I assumed it was used to keep my mouth open, but I never asked. A man in a white lab coat then asked me to count backward, starting at ten. I think I got to seven.

When I woke up, I was screaming and crying. I didn't know why. The next thing I noticed

was some gauze in my mouth and my teeth hurting
very badly. I looked over and saw my mother, and
I realized I was alive, and it was over. I tried to
calm myself down. Soon after, we were allowed to
go home. I stayed home the next three days and
just watched TV.

The following Sunday, Stan asked me to go
waterskiing, so I decided my mouth was finally
better. I waited on the end of Gramps' dock for
Stan and his father to come by in their 20-foot
speed boat to pick me up. Stan's father had been
involved in my past three seasons of baseball and
two seasons of basketball either as head coach or
assistant coach, so I referred to him as Coach.
Coach had just bought the speed boat
earlier this summer. We had skied five times and
progressed in our ability to waterski each time.
The first time, Stan and I struggled to get up on
two skis, but eventually we both made it and skied
around Upper Straits Lake. As soon as we got
comfortable, we were able to ski in and out of the
wake. Our third time out, we learned to drop a ski
and move in and out of the wake on one ski. We
had so much fun alternating turns while Coach
drove the boat. The last time out, we'd both tried
to get up on one ski. Stan got up the first time he
tried. It took me several attempts, but after I got
up the first time, I had it down like riding a bike. I
really enjoyed the feeling of gliding across the
water.
As the boat approached, Stan threw out the
bumpers to ensure the boat didn't hit the dock. I
put out my arms to help guide the boat close to the

dock without damage. I got in the boat and helped push away from the dock.

"How's The Machine? Seen Rocky lately?" said Stan.

"Hello, Tom," said Coach.

"Hey, The Man. Hi, Coach. I think Rocky is getting ready for football season."

We didn't tell our parents that Rocky was a girl. We used her name as joke when we were around parents.

"Who's going first?" said Coach.

"Stan, you go. I want to see how The Man does it."

Stan put on the life vest and jumped in. I floated the slalom ski to him. Coach tied the rope to the boat and threw the handle to Stan, who was putting on the ski.

"Stan, ready for me to let the slack out?" Coach yelled.

"All set."

After the rope became taut, Stan started dragging as the boat was idling.

"Hit it!" Stan yelled.

Coach pushed the throttle down. Stan teetered a little and got a face full of water, but after about three seconds, he was up and skiing. Stan started weaving in and out of the wake but not giving the big spray that you see with experienced water skiers.

"Coach, how do you get the big spray?" I asked.

"Well, Tom, once you get all the way out to one side, lean back and at the same time lean toward the wake."

I had grown accustomed to Coach giving me instructions, and they were usually very helpful.

"Thanks, Coach."

Stan smiled at me as he did some maneuvers and finally got tired. He put his hands in the air as he let go of the rope. By putting his hands in the air, he was letting me know that he didn't fall and was going down on his own.

"He's down," I told Coach.

Coach immediately turned around and went to pick up Stan. Stan scooted the ski toward the boat, and I reached in and picked it up. Then he climbed into the boat, took off his life vest, and grabbed a towel.

"You are The Man. Good job," I told him.

"Let's see if you can weave in and out like me," Stan challenged.

The competition was on. I put on the life vest and jumped in. The water was very calm today and like a sheet of glass. This is how we liked it. The sun was shining, and it didn't take us long to dry off when we got in the boat. Stan floated the ski toward me, and I put it on. I grabbed the rope, and Coach started moving the boat away in idle.

"Hit   it."

After a few seconds, I was out of the water and skiing on one ski. I then started going in and out of the wake like Stan did. As I went all the way to the right, I decided I wanted to try to spray, so I leaned back and to the left. I could feel the spray as I rocketed toward the wake. But as I hit the wake, my ski came out of the water and the only part of me touching the water was my head and shoulder as the rope jerked from my hands and my ski came off. As I came up, I could feel some pain, and it felt like the wind was knocked out of me. I tried to maneuver toward the ski and the boat approached.

"Tom, great spray," Stan yelled.

"Are you okay?" said Coach.

"I think I'm okay, but I better come in the boat and rest."

I pushed the ski toward the boat, and Stan picked it up. I then climbed up the ladder.

"Wow, what an awesome spray and great wipeout!"

I tried to smile and not show my pain.

"How did you get that spray?"

"Well, I leaned back and over, but I may have leaned over a bit too much."

"Oh, I can't wait to try it."

Stan then went for another ski run and of course, had to try to spray to keep up with me. He didn't get the spray that I did, but he did fall over. His fall was not nearly as bad as mine. He decided to try it again. Coach got him up again and this time he was able to spray a little and stay up. After his run, Coach asked me if I was ready to go again. Still hurting a little, I really didn't know, but I told him that I was.

I got out of the water and started weaving in and out of the wake. Each time I leaned back and to the side a little as I cut back to the wake. I was getting a medium spray. At the end of the run, I let go of the ski rope handle and put my arms in the air in triumph. We each took one more run and they dropped me off near Gramps' raft so I could swim to shore.

"Thanks, Stan. Thanks, Coach. See you soon."

"Don't forget to sign up for the Red Devils."

The Red Devils was the name of the local football league. Since becoming friends with Stan during baseball season two years ago, I'd also played football with him for two years. I played right defensive end and had gotten pretty good at it. Stan played wingback and right outside linebacker. Since we were going into the seventh grade, we could have played on the junior high team, but there we would have to compete with the bigger eighth grade boys. The Red Devils went up to age 12, and since we were both 12 years old we could still play and be the older boys on the team. There was one other restriction. The Red Devils had a weight restriction of 120 pounds with pads. For Stan, this was no problem, but for me, 120 pounds was pushing it. Still, I thought I could stay under the weight.

I swam to where I could touch, walked in the rest of the way and headed home. When I got there, my mother was on the phone, which was typical for her. When she got off the phone she came and told me we needed to go to a funeral on Tuesday. I'd only been to one funeral: when I was 5 years old for an older Hungarian immigrant I didn't know.

"Who died?"

"Anna. She's your second cousin. You may not remember her because it has been a while since you saw her. She was 10 years old."

"Wow, what happened?"

"She was playing hide and seek using the front door of a neighbor's house as free. She ran right through the storm door, which was a full pane of glass."

"Wow! That's awful!"

This certainly was an awful situation, and was the first truly awful experience I'd heard about since I started thinking about awful as being hit over the head with a baseball bat. I didn't really remember who she was because I had many

31

second cousins whose parents had all come from Hungary. But even though I didn't know her, I felt sad. I had so many dreams and it was sad to think they could be taken away by such a freak accident. I had just had a bad fall skiing. Could it have been me? I felt lucky that I had survived that fall. I was doing something very daring. All Anna did was play hide and go seek. It hit me hard and I couldn't stop thinking about her.

"When I die and they lay me to rest,
Going to go to the place that's the best.
When they lay me down to die,
Going up to the Spirit in the Sky."
— Norman Greenbaum (1969)

Hungarian Family

"**M**om, I'm not going to wear a tie. It chokes me."

"Tom, I don't ask you to do a lot, but we will be seeing a lot of people and the tie is a show of respect."

"Do you want me to be strangled?"

"I could have asked you to cut your hair. I'm sure some people are going to think I'm raising a hippie freak."

My hair wasn't really that long for 1970. It covered my ears and my forehead but only came to my shoulders. Some boys were wearing their hair down their back. My mother tolerated my desire for longer hair but she certainly didn't like it.

"No, no! Not my hair!"

"Tom, how is a clip-on tie going to choke you?"

"It's buttoning the top button that chokes me."

"I would really appreciate it if you would do this for me. You're going to see a lot of our family and people from the old country."

I finally gave in to my mother's wishes and wore a tie. My mother drove to the funeral home. I was afraid to see a dead body of someone close to my age. It seemed like a cruel thing to make me see her this way.

As we walked into the funeral home, everyone seemed to recognize my mother. It seemed that she was one of the few Hungarian immigrants who moved away from city.

"*Jó napot*," I heard as I walked in. This is a Hungarian greeting for good day.

My mother greeted and hugged everyone speaking to some in English and some in Hungarian. My mother introduced me to everyone. At first I responded to the Hungarian greetings with "Hi," but after my mother gave me a pointed look, I started responding with "*jó napot.*"

As I was talking to my grandparents, I noticed my mother talking to a man. Both were smiling and laughing. Based on the pictures I had seen, I suspected this man was my father. After their conversation, she walked back over to me.

"Is that him?" I asked.

"Yes, Tom, that man is your father."

"Why didn't he come over to meet me?"

"I don't know. We should go view the body now."

This puzzled me. Why wouldn't he want to talk to his own flesh and blood?

We walked toward the open casket. Even though I only looked for about two seconds, seeing Anna lying there really bothered me. She looked all pale and was wearing horned-rim glasses.

I started having a bunch of thoughts. I wanted to live forever. Why do people have to die? I want to live every year. I want to be here in the year 2000. Wow, I will be 42 years old then. I will look ancient. I want to live. I've spent 12 years accumulating knowledge. I can't imagine this knowledge just going away.

The funeral started, but I kept thinking about life. I didn't really know Anna, but I knew she was someone who was too young to die. I looked around and saw my father sitting in the back of the funeral home. Why hadn't he ever wanted to meet me? Why wouldn't he be excited to see me today?

As we were leaving the funeral home, I looked for my father and thought he had left—but then I saw him. I left my mother and walked over to him.

"*Hogy vagy*?" I said to my father. This means "how are you?" in Hungarian. I was trying to follow my mother's wishes to be polite and say something in Hungarian.

"Oh, hi," he responded quietly, making no attempt to answer me in Hungarian.

Since he didn't have much to say, I decided to talk about the one thing I knew well, myself.

"Did my mother tell you I play three sports now? I did really well in basketball. I was on the city all-star baseball team. This fall, I am playing football. I play defensive end and quarterback."

At least I plan to try to play quarterback this year, I thought but didn't want to say.

His response was simply, "Oh, real good, real good."

"Maybe you could come see me play sometime."

He didn't say anything. So I started to walk back to my mother, but I turned and said, "*köszönöm*," the Hungarian word for thank you.

This was not the conversation I had dreamt of having with my father. He didn't seem that interested in me, and I didn't understand why. I didn't say a lot on the drive home, but the brief conversation with my father had distracted me from the trauma of seeing a girl lying dead. Why was the last thing I said to him in Hungarian when the first time I spoke Hungarian he responded in English? Looking back, if I would have said a simple thank you in English, it might have been more respectful. I was confused. Other fathers are involved in their son's lives and many come to every game their sons play.

Even though my father wasn't interested in me, I have a mother who goes to every one of my games. She's very interested in me. I also have three men in my life who are very interested in me: Gramps has been wonderful and has taught me many things about life that most fathers couldn't teach their sons. Coach has helped me so much in sports. There's also Grandpa Mochina, who has helped me appreciate sports from the fan's point of view. All three men have accepted me just like one of their own children. I enjoy my time with all three of them, but being with my actual father was very awkward. I don't have a father in my home, but I have a special mother and three very special men.

I finally asked my mother about this. "I saw you laughing with my father, but he didn't seem too interested in me. Why?"

"Your father told me I looked gorgeous and wanted to know if I wanted to go out with him again. I told him maybe he could come to one of your football games this fall. He told me he just wanted it to be him and me. Tom, he doesn't want a relationship with me or you. He just wants to be with me for a while and then...well, let's just say he has commitment issues. You're a large part of my life, and if he wants to be with me, he must be with you too."

No wonder he didn't answer when I invited him to a game.

"Mom, thanks for telling me this."

The next day was Wednesday, and it was my morning to work with Gramps. I went down to the lake, sat on the chair on his dock and looked out on the water. After a little while, Gramps walked up.

"Tom, I got bad news for you."

Oh, no, what else?

"The grass didn't stay mowed, and the boats didn't stay clean."

I smiled. "Gramps, I went to a funeral yesterday for a 10-year-old girl who died running through a pane-glass door."

"Oh, that must have been really hard."

"It was very hard, but instead of thinking about her, I started thinking about myself and how I want to live. I was very worried about the dental surgery. I want to see the year 2000."

"Tom, you will see the year 2000, but I won't. I would be 92 in the year 2000. I won't be here."

"Gramps, you'll be here. I'll come out to your dock that summer, and you'll talk to me."

"Tom, we are only placed on earth for a short time. Unfortunately, some of us are here a shorter time than others, like the girl you saw today. It's not how long you live, but how you live. My life has been very rewarding. I've been able to help a lot of people as a physician and an instructor. I got to meet a lot of special people along the way, and you are certainly one of the most special people in my life. If I die tomorrow, I can say that my life is complete. However, if I live for many more years, I'm going to spend them helping more people enjoy life and enjoying the peace of this lake. You were born 50 years after me and will hopefully live 50 or more years after I die."

"Gramps, I want to live forever."

"Tom, you might, but no one has so far. It's not pleasant to think about our own death. It's more pleasant to think about our hopes and dreams for the current year. I don't think about the year 2000. I think about what I can do in 1970. Tom, someday, someone closer to you will die, and it will be normal to be sad for a while and grieve this person, but then after time has passed, you should accept the death and live your life and fulfill your own dreams."

"*Köszönöm.*"

"What did you call me?" Gramps said with a scowl and then smiled.

I smiled. "Thanks, Gramps. Let's get those chores done."

After I washed the boats, moved the picnic table and picked up the sticks and walnuts for Gramps, I rowed down to meet Stan. I was certainly getting stronger from all of the rowing.

When I got to Stan's beach, I didn't see him, but I did see Rocky and Danny. They were sitting on their beach blanket with a couple of older guys. The guys were probably in high school and were much bigger than me. I watched for a while and saw Rocky laughing with the guys when Stan walked up.

"You are the rowing machine," he said. "You made great time."

At first I didn't say anything. I shut my eyes, put my upper teeth behind my lower teeth and started to breathe. I'm sure Stan could tell something was wrong. He'd seen that look on me before. He started looking around and saw Danny and Rocky with the two guys and looked back at me.

"Would you be really disappointed if I didn't stay today?" I asked.

"Tom, I get it. Call me when you want to get together."

I pushed the boat off and started rowing back. I rowed really hard, and it helped me take out my frustrations. I felt really hurt that Rocky was with another guy. But who was I trying to kid? I didn't have a shot with a girl two years older than me. I guess she had fun babysitting me until a real man came along. I realized that I had fallen for a lady who was out of my reach. I felt really stupid.

I felt a little calmer when I got back to the dock. I tied the boat up hung up the cushions and started to walk home. Gramps saw me and probably knew I wasn't happy, so he didn't say anything. I was not fair to Stan by not staying when I was upset. Luckily he was very understanding. But I wasn't going to just walk by Gramps too.

"Gramps!"

"Tom! Short trip."

"I saw something that bothered me, and I left. I was not fair to Stan, who had come to meet me, but I just really got a jealous, angry feeling when I saw Rocky talking to an older guy."

"Rocky?"

I smiled. I'm sure Gramps thought Rocky was a guy. "Rocky is the girl I've been talking to down at Stan's beach." I laughed. "Gramps, I figured it out on the way home: Rocky is a very pretty ninth grader. Of course she should talk to high school guys. Somehow I was expecting her to want to talk to me today."

"It has been a rough week for you. Sometimes things just get to us, especially if we've had had other stressors in our life."

"I was able to resolve this on my way back to the dock. Rocky is not going to be my girlfriend. I'm okay with that. What I really feel bad about is that I left Stan. He's so good to me, and he looked like he understood as I left. But I should be a better friend to him. He might have been hurt too, seeing Danny talking to an older guy. I was selfish. I need to be a better friend."

"Tom, you've got it figured out. If something happens we don't like, it's really okay to feel bad. I would surely feel bad if some older guy took my girlfriend."

I laughed and shook my head. Gramps didn't have to worry about guys much older than him. "Gramps, she wasn't my girlfriend. I liked her a lot and found her really good looking. I think she was my girlfriend in my dreams only. Thanks."

When I got home, I called Stan and apologized for leaving.

"Hey, I would've never got to hang out with two babes like that if it wasn't for you. I know if I hang around you, the girls will come crawling," Stan said, and then we both started laughing.

"Let's get together tomorrow and throw that football one more time before practice starts."

I agreed to meet him. Stan was a great friend. He puts up with me.

The next day I met Stan at the beach, and it was a little cooler than normal so not many people were there. There was no sign of Rocky and Danny.

Defensive End

"Ooo-oh Child,
Things are going to get easier.
Ooo-oh Child,
Things will get brighter."
— The Five Stair Steps (1970)

A Slight Edge

T he football season was my next life journey. The league was divided by area, and Stan and I lived in the area for the Red Devils. The Red Devils consisted of players between the ages of 9 and 12. I didn't play when I was 9 years old, but I had played the last two seasons. There were three divisions based on age and weight: freshman, JV, and varsity. I played JV at age 10 and varsity last year, so this season would be my second at the varsity level. This was a much better option than playing with the eighth graders on the junior high school team where I might not get to play much.

I'd established myself as a fairly good defensive end last year after learning the position the year before. I'd also established myself as a tough kid who wasn't afraid to "put a helmet on someone." Leading with your helmet is discouraged today, but back in 1970, the best players led with their heads.

Stan played outside linebacker on the same side as me: the right side. It was our job to make sure we shut down anything coming to our side of the field. Stan also got to play some offense—he got to carry the ball. Stan had very good speed, and if he got an opening, he could run a long way.

At the end of last season, I had expressed to Coach Patterson that I wanted to play quarterback. He gave me some sheets of paper showing the plays and told me what to practice. I was excited to show him how hard I'd worked to become a very good quarterback. Our quarterback from last year was now thirteen and would have to play for the junior high school, so as far as I knew, the starting quarterback job was up for grabs.

The first two weeks of practice were during the day, so my mother couldn't take me due to her job. Coach was also at work, so my mother arranged for the other mothers of kids on the team to take me to practice. Some of these players and parents had never seen my house before. I was worried that they might say something about how small it was. However, the only comment I ever got was how great it must be to have the woods and lake so close.

The first two days of practice were without pads or helmets. At the first practice, Coach Patterson had me run some quarterback drills along with Kevin, the second-team quarterback from last year. Most of the plays were running plays but there were a few pass plays. I was much bigger than Kevin, and I think I outplayed him in all of the drills. I started feeling pretty confident that I would be the quarterback of the team.

We ran an I-formation with two tight ends and a wingback. Most of the time, we either ran the crossbuck or the quarterback option. We also had a reverse to the wingback if the defense was over-pursuing or, as we called it, wasn't "staying home." The number in the play calling was either at 3 (over right tackle), 4 (over right guard), 6 (over left guard), or 7 (over left tackle). So the play "crossbuck at 4" meant that I gave the ball to the fullback over right guard, then faked to the halfback toward over left tackle, and then I rolled out to the right. "crossbuck at 7" was the same play, only I faked to the fullback and gave to the halfback. "Crossbuck at 7 – pass" was the same play, only I would fake to both, roll out and either run or throw a pass to the wingback or a tight end, all of whom faked a block and ran a pass pattern. "Crossbuck at 6," "crossbuck at 3," and crossbuck at 3 – pass" were the same plays going the other way.

Our other main play was "quarterback option right" (or left). On this play, I would fake to the fullback over right guard (if I gave it to him, that play was "Dive at 4"), then I would come down the line and decide to either run it myself, pitch to the tailback or pass it to the wingback, who first blocked and then slipped the block into a pass pattern. I thought I was good at running this the option because I could make smart decisions to run, pass or pitch. Being one of the bigger boys, if I decided to run, I was hard to tackle without gaining another 2 or 3 yards when I fell forward.

On Wednesday of the first week of practice we were issued our equipment. We stood in a line first to get our shoulder pads and helmets. Then we stood in a line to get our pants and a girdle. The pants came equipped with two knee pads and two thigh pads. The girdle went on before the pants and looked like oversized underwear with five pads: two pads on each side and the tailbone pad in the back. We had to get good at putting our pads in our pants and girdle because each time they were washed, the pads had to come out and then be put back. It was quite a chore. Lastly, we got our jerseys. Kevin had already been through the line and got quarterback jersey number 10. But I got the jersey number I wanted: number 11. I'd now worn number 11 for three seasons of baseball and two seasons of basketball, so it was my number of choice. Since I mainly played defensive end, I'd worn numbers 51 and 55 the past two seasons in football. One of the quarterbacks battling for the starting job for the Detroit Lions, Greg Landry, wore number 11, so it worked out very well.

During one practice later that week, I was playing defensive end, and the tight end, Bill, was having a very difficult time trying to block me. I was getting into the backfield and disrupting almost every play. The coaches were not pleased with the job Bill was doing and were trying to give him instruction on how to block me. After some time, I could tell Bill was frustrated. But he still had to execute his block. I was out there trying to show what I could do, and I was not going to make it easy on him. On the next play, I shot the gap between the tight end and the tackle and tackled the quarterback before he was able to execute the play. As I tried to get up I could feel a facemask hit me in the back. I turned around and saw Bill. I grabbed his facemask and pulled his face to the ground, making sure he hit hard.

The coach had seen what had happened. On the football field, retaliation is often rewarded. The coach told me how tough I was, but then said that if this had been a game, I would have gotten a 15-yard penalty. He asked me to find a way to retaliate legally. I understood his point, but this was one time I didn't feel bad about trying to hurt someone. Bill had struck me with his helmet, in the back, when I was down. I felt fine about how

I'd handled the situation. I enjoyed playing football. I could once again hit people and yet not go to the principal's office.

At the start of the second week of practice, the coach divided the offense into Red Offense and White Offense and the defense into Red Defense and White Defense. I was assigned to Red Defense and White Offense, while Stan was on both Red Offense and Red Defense. It didn't take us long to figure out that the Red teams were the first teams and the White teams were the second teams. In this football league, the second teams were required to play four plays each half and, in general, the first teams played the rest of the plays.

I was certainly not happy about being the second-team quarterback. I didn't understand why the coach had made this decision. Was my mother right? Because I didn't live with a father, I again wasn't chosen to be the starter? I didn't smile that practice, and I probably hit a little harder than I had to hit to execute the plays. When I did get my chance to play quarterback, I wanted to make sure I played well, so I tried to put my frustration behind me.

Now that Stan had been my friend for more than two years, he knew by looking at me that I was frustrated, and he also knew there wasn't a lot he could say to cheer me up. After practice, Stan asked me to come to his house for a while. He told me he was excited that we'd be on the same side of the field on defense and play at the same time again this year, but he was very disappointed that I wouldn't get to be his quarterback. He said I was much better and should've been chosen as the starter. I felt a little better hearing him say this.

—◆—

The week went on, and I continued to run the second-team offense to the best of my ability. On Saturday, I stopped down to talk to Gramps.

"Tommy Boy, I've missed you. I didn't get the boats cleaned this week."

"Hi, Gramps," I said with a smile. "I would be happy to help you now."

"What's a man do standing up, a woman sitting down, and a dog on three legs?"

The answer seemed obvious but I just couldn't answer. "Hmmm, I'm not sure."

"Shake hands," replied Gramps. "It is customary that a man stand up to shake hands while a woman can remain seated."

I laughed because it was not the answer I expected but I learned something I did not know that would help me later in life.

As we started cleaning the boats, Gramps asked me how football was going.

"Gramps, I thought I was playing very well. I'm going to start at right defensive end, but I'm going to run the second team at quarterback." I was not enthusiastic at all and frowned as I spoke.

"Tom, wow—that's great. Do you know how many boys dream of playing quarterback, but only two or three on each team get to play that position. I'm excited for you."

"Gramps, I was good enough to start, but politics must've gotten in the way."

"Tom, did the guy who's playing quarterback with the first team play quarterback last year?"

"Yes, Kevin was the second-team quarterback last year."

"Tom, quarterback is a position that can make or break a team. It's important to have someone playing it with some experience. I bet your coach wants to see how you perform in a game situation before he awards you the starting position. With Kevin, he knows what he's going to get. With you, even though you do well in practice, he doesn't know what he's going to get in a game situation. You're going to have to show him your game skills before he promotes you."

"Gramps, that makes sense, but I wanted to start."

"Tom, football coaches want to win. If you show him that he has a better chance of winning with you at quarterback, he'll play you. He doesn't care about your family, your family's income, or whether or not you have long hair. He wants to gain victories."

As usual, Gramps had the answer. He made me laugh with a comment about my hair. It was hard for older people to understand why I wanted longer hair. I've been so lucky to have him in my life. Someday, I'm going to help others the same way Gramps has helped me.

When I got home, there was a large custom red van in the yard. When I entered the house, I saw a man with dark, slicked back hair and dark eyes sitting on the couch. My mother introduced him to me.

"Tom, this is Vito. Vito is Italian. Vito, this is my son, Tom."

"Tom, I've heard so much about you. I heard you don't let anyone push you around."

I found this an odd thing for him to say. He could have said anything positive. My mother's statements were weird too. Why would the first thing she said about him be that he is Italian?

"I'm really good at standing my ground when it's needed," I said with a scowl.

Vito then told me all about himself and how good he was at pretty much everything. He also told me about his daughter, who was a year older than me, and his son, who was a year younger than me, and how great they both were at everything. My mother seemed amazed by this man.

After a while he finally asked something about me. It was regarding football.

"I'm the starting quarterback and defensive end. We went undefeated last year."

My mother's face dropped. We actually only won two of nine games, and this was going to be the first year I played quarterback. She started to say something, but Vito interrupted her so she was never able to correct me.

"I'm going to start dinner," she finally said.

"My son played quarterback last year, but he was too big and tough, so the coach asked him to move to middle linebacker," commented Vito.

I was thinking the man was making up his story. His son didn't move from quarterback to defense because he was too big and tough. Vito was trying to talk negatively about my position. Did he even have a son?

"What team does your son play for?"

"He's on the Wolverines. They have blue and yellow helmets like the University of Michigan."

I doubted there was a little league team called the Wolverines. My mother must have told him I liked the Michigan State Spartans, so he was simply saying this to be negative.

"What city?"

"Madison Heights. My son and daughter go to St. Dennis Catholic School but will go to Bishop Foley for high school."

I had the comeback for his comment, and I could bring my mother with me. "My mother and I are Protestant and very proud of it." I was starting to feel like this was an argument. He wasn't winning me over at all.

We ate dinner. My mother doesn't normally make spaghetti, but she decided to make it that night. I guess she thought Italian food would be appropriate. I tried to keep quiet during dinner, and when dinner ended, I got up from the table.

"Mom, your spaghetti was very good, but there's nothing better than your Hungarian goulash. *Köszönöm.* I'm going to watch TV. *Let's Make a Deal* is starting."

"*Köszönöm*, Tom."

"I like the *Andy Williams Show*, and it's starting too," said Vito.

I looked at my mother. We had one TV. "I'll go play in my room."

—✦—

On Sunday, I went down to Gramps' beach for a swim even though my mother thought the water was getting cold. It was August 30. Normally, you can swim in August, but not in September, so I was determined to take my last swim of the year. When I got down there, I noticed Gramps and his son, Charlie, were pulling the raft in. I swam out to see if I could help.

"Charlie, here comes a strong young man to help you out," said Gramps, smiling.

"Hi, Gramps! Hi, Charlie!"

51

"Tom, I need your help," said Charlie.

Charlie was a big guy. I don't think he really needed my help, but I was happy that he asked me. The water was a little chilly, but I didn't want to show I was cold. When I got to the raft, Charlie gave me a rope, and I helped him pull. At that point, Gramps was just rowing a boat alongside us. When we got to shore, Gramps got his tractor to pull the raft away from the water while Charlie and I helped guide it.

"Tom, your timing was great as usual. Labor Day is not until September 7 this year. Last year it was on September 1, so decided to not wait until Labor Day to bring the raft to shore."

Although it was new to celebrate Memorial Day on a Monday, Labor Day had been on Monday for some time.

"Tom, Charlie played football."

"What position did you play?" I asked him.

"I mainly played tight end and defensive end. I played the right defensive end so I could sack the right-handed quarterback from the blind side," Charlie said with a huge smile.

"Charlie, I would love for you to teach me some points about the position."

Charlie then taught me many things I could use. He taught me to tackle by hitting the opponent low and then wrapping him up with my arms. He taught me how to shed a blocker so I would be ready to tackle the ball carrier.

"Fight pressure with pressure." Charlie explained that if a blocker is trying to push me in a certain direction, I should try to go the opposite way.

"Tom, remember that the difference between good and great is a slight edge." Charlie held up his right hand with his thumb and index finger about 1 inch apart. "If you can give this much more than the opponent, you'll win."

I'm not sure I totally understood this at the time, but I remembered it and thought about it every time I played football.

Charlie was a nice guy. Why did he have to be married? I wished my mother could meet a man like him. He and my mother were the same age, but he had waited longer to have children. Charlie and his wife now had a three-year-old son, Ray, Jr., and a one-year-old daughter, Wendy. Charlie must have really liked his father to name his firstborn son after him.

"Charlie, I really appreciate your help. Are you going to come to a game this fall?"

"I'll try to. I'm not sure how long Ray and Wendy will be able to be there without fussing."

"Charlie, you and Sue go to a game. Ruth and I will be happy to watch Ray and Wendy," responded Gramps.

We all smiled and said our goodbyes. I hadn't said anything about Vito. I preferred to talk with Gramps about problems when it was just the two of us.

Defensive End

Breaking the Law

We had one more week of practice before the scrimmage against our crosstown rivals, the Blue Devils. We also had one more week before the start of school. Monday after football practice, my mother wanted to take me clothes shopping to get ready. She took me to the Pontiac Mall. The thing I liked most about going to the mall was stopping at Arby's on the way.

Ordering at Arby's was as much fun as eating because the cashiers were black, and they had microphones to announce the order as it was being placed. Being at Arby's and the Pontiac Mall were about the only times I came in contact with black people. I couldn't even get the words out of my mouth before the cashier would repeat them in the microphone.

"I'll take a regular Ar—"

"ARBYS," roared the guy into the microphone.

"And French fri—"

"FRIES."

"And I'll have an orange pop."

"ORANGE."

I enjoyed my meal and put a lot of Arby's sauce on my sandwich.

The Pontiac Mall was the first indoor mall built in the Detroit area and attracted a lot of people. In the middle of the mall was a Kresge store. This store was my favorite because Kresge had all of the latest toys. The Kresge Company had already started a new concept of just using the K and having standalone K-Mart stores. My mother said she had to get a few things at a women's store, Winkleman's, so I looked around Kresge's. She'd told me she would meet me at the fountain in the middle of the mall so after looking at some toys, I went there to wait for her.

There were coins in the fountain and a younger boy was reaching in and taking some of them. Being a coin collector, I started to wonder if there were some old coins in there. The boy looked at me and told me I could reach in and get some coins if I wanted. When I hesitated, he told me the coins were there for people to take, and if they didn't want people taking them, they would lock the area. Somehow I took this as permission, so I reached in and grabbed two pennies and started to look at them. Just then, a policeman walked up and asked what I was doing. I explained to him that another boy had told me I could reach in and grab some coins if I wanted, so I was going to look to see if there were any older pennies. When I went to point to the other boy, he was gone.

"That's stealing. I should take you in," the policeman said.

Stealing? Take me in? I started to get really scared. I didn't want to go to jail. I'd been taught at church that stealing was wrong, and I would never want to steal.

"I'm really sorry. I had no idea. The boy told me it was okay. I certainly didn't mean to steal. Please don't take me away."

"Yeah, right. I've heard that one before. Where are your parents?"

"My mother should be here any minute. She'll tell you."

He didn't believe me. Why not? I'm very honest. Just then my mother walked up.

"Ma'am, is this your son?"

"Yes sir. Is there a problem?"

"I caught him stealing money from the fountain. It looks like he only took two pennies, so I'm going to have him throw them back. Make sure he learns stealing is wrong."

"Yes, sir."

The police officer walked away.

"Tom, what were you thinking?" my mother asked.

"I thought it was okay. I saw another boy doing it."

"It's never okay to steal. I'm so disappointed in you. You're lucky he didn't take you to jail."

It seemed that no one understood this was just a mistake, and I really didn't mean to steal. I was upset with both my mother and the police officer. They should have known I was telling the truth.

There were two main stores in the mall where you could buy children's clothes: Hudson's and Montgomery Ward. My mother thought Hudson's was more expensive, so she took me to Montgomery Ward—or just Ward's as we called it back then. Shopping with my mother was not a pleasant experience. She preferred to get it done quickly. She would pick up a shirt and ask if I liked it. Of course, I usually didn't.

"Mom, I can't wear any of these. I need something mod."

"Mod?"

"Yes, I need colorful shirts and bell-bottom jeans."

After shopping a while, I found some clothes that were within my mother's budget and that I thought would look cool. We got back home with some new school clothes, and I was happy that I had avoided going to jail.

On Thursday night, Vito came over again in his custom van. I tried to avoid him as much as possible, but it didn't take long for him to say something to me.

"Hey, Tom, do you like the Minnesota Vikings?"

"Of course not. I live in Michigan. I'm a Detroit Lions fan."

"I like the Vikings. They won the division last year and will win it again. They have a great defense, the Purple People Eaters!"

"The Detroit Lions have a much-improved team. This is 1970 and not 1969. It's a new season. Don't you live in Michigan?"

"I live in Michigan, but I prefer the best team, and that team's the Vikings."

"We'll see about that when they play each other."

I could tell my mother really liked this guy. I couldn't figure it out. He seemed like the total opposite of her. I decided to hang out in my room and listen to some rock and roll. I had bought the 45 of "Signs" by the Five Man Electrical Band and decided to play it and sing along.

"And the sign said you got to have a membership card to get inside, ugh."

On Saturday, I ventured down to Gramps' place to sit on his dock. He was out.

"Tommy?"

"Hey, Gramps. How are you?"

"Did you hear about the woman who dressed up as a man and got into the army? Of course, there was only one shower room, so the men could all tell she was a woman, but no one reported her."

I laughed and laughed. I'm not sure if it was that funny or if I was laughing at hearing Gramps tell a story about a naked lady.

"My mother's been captured by the mafia."

"Okay, Tom, what's the punch line?"

"Unfortunately it's not a joke. There's this Italian guy who comes over in his custom van, and my mother drools over him."

"Tom, it's hard on your mother. She needs some adult company."

"Gramps, I don't like this guy. He tries to argue everything. He likes the Vikings!"

"Wow, the Vikings! Oh well, let him like the Vikings. The Lions get to play them twice this year, and we'll find out who the better team is."

"Gramps, he thinks Michigan will beat Michigan State."

"I really hope he's wrong about that one, but Michigan has a good team this year. That will be a very tough game for the Spartans."

"I just don't like him."

"Tom, some people use negativity for humor. It's not my style, and I know it's not yours. But if your mother likes him and he's going to spend time at the house, it might be best if you could get along with him on some level. You might want to talk to your mother about him."

"I will. Just knowing he's coming over gets me worked up."

"So you're anticipating how bad he will be before he even comes over?"

"Yes. So far he's been negative every time."

"If you're thinking the interaction will be bad before you see him, it will be bad. Try giving him a chance. He sounds like a different guy than you're used to being around. He's not going to think like you. He's going to think like him. You'd be able to tolerate him more if you expected him to act like him. The water is so peaceful today. Are you going for a swim?"

I went over and stood in the water about ankle deep.

"I think I'll wait until next spring. But I'm excited about the football scrimmage tomorrow."

"Tom, I hope you do well. I'll be excited to hear about it."

"Thanks, Gramps."

The next day, my mother took me to the Walled Lake Western High School football field where we played all of our home games. Before the game, we had to weigh in with all of our pads. I was one of the heaviest players, mainly because I was one of the tallest. I weighed in at 115 pounds.

The coach told me that if I weighed in at over 120, I would not be eligible to play.

We loosened up with some calisthenics and ran a few plays. I was excited for the scrimmage to start. I thought about what plays I would make on defense. I also thought about playing quarterback for the first time and how I was planning on doing very well. I thought about all the people watching who would get to see how good I was.

Since this was a scrimmage, there were no kickoffs. The scrimmage started with our first-team offense, which did not include me, at the 50-yard line. They didn't move the ball at all. They got to run 10 plays before the switch was made to have our first-team defense come out.

I stepped on the field for the first time. On the third play, the other team ran the ball my way, and I tackled the ball carrier at the line of scrimmage. I could hear over the loud speaker, "Johnson, the ball carrier, brought down for no gain by Moe-China." I couldn't believe they'd gotten my name wrong. They were saying it like the country and not like Sheena. I'm sure others thought this was funny, and I really felt disrespected. On the next play, they threw a pass, and it was completed for a touchdown.

They ended up scoring again in their 10 plays, but then it was my turn to go in and play quarterback with the second-team offense. The coach had told me what plays to run, but I got to choose the order. I enjoyed calling the plays in the huddle. I decided to start with the crossbuck at 6, and that play was stopped for no gain. I came back with crossbuck at 3, and we gained 2 yards. On third down with 9 yards to go, I called my own number: the quarterback sneak on a quick count. I ran for 4 yards and fell forward for 2 more.

"Moe-China, the ball carrier, brought down after a gain of 6 by Burns."

I got up and thought about my next play. They were probably looking for the quarterback sneak again, but I decided to call the option right.

I looked at my wingback Fred and said, "Get ready!"

The ball was snapped, and as I came down the line, I saw Fred open. I threw him the ball and he ran for about 10 more yards.

"Mahoney on a pass from Moe-China for 15 yards and a first down, pushed out of bounds by Valentine."

It was the longest play from scrimmage for our team so far. I was ready to go back and try the crossbuck the other way when reality struck: The first-team offense was running out on the field. I just showed I could move the offense, but it didn't matter. The reality was that the second team got four plays a half, and my four plays were over.

As I came off the field, Coach Patterson said, "Tom, good job out there."

I looked at him but didn't say anything. Stan and I continued to make some tackles on defense, but this team was clearly better than us. In the second half, I got my four plays at quarterback. I again had a nice run of 5 yards, but this time threw an incomplete pass and we were not able to get a first down. Officially there was no score kept, but we knew that the Blue Devils had scored three touchdowns, and we had scored none. I'd had my mispronounced name called for three tackles.

After the game, I wasn't too happy, but I did ask my mother if she would go to the press box before every game and tell them to pronounce my name the right way. When I got home, I wrote down my statistics for the game.

"It's a little bit funny this feeling inside.
I'm not one of those who could easily hide.
I don't have much money but boy if I did,
I'd buy a big house where we both could live."
— *Elton John (1970)*

History Lesson

The day after the first game was Labor Day, and my mother wanted to spend it with her parents, Grandpa and Grandma Mochina, so we drove to the city. A few other relatives were also over, and although there wasn't anyone my age, one of my mother's cousins, Rod, was in the 11th grade at Birmingham Groves High School. He was a drummer in a local rock band. I had a good time talking and playing games with him. He had longer hair than I did. He also had a talent for art and liked to make posters. He told me that two years ago when the Tigers were in the World Series, he made posters and went down to Tiger Stadium and sold them.

Much of the adult conversation revolved around the funeral. Everyone was still stunned by what had happened to Anna. Since I had football to think about, I hadn't thought much more about Anna, but I did when I heard her being talked about. I thought about her lying there lifeless. I just couldn't imagine that being me. I was so happy I still had my life.

Grandpa was outside with Rod and me. I asked him if he'd talked to my father at the funeral.

He looked at me for a minute and just said, "No, I did not. I will never forgive him for leaving your mother when she was pregnant."

I could tell he didn't want to talk about him.

When I went inside, my mother was telling Rod's mother, my Aunt Dot, about Vito. She smiled as she talked about him.

My grandma called me for dinner. I sat down and noticed the glasses made of real glass. I know this is not unusual, but it was for me since we normally used plastic. I felt really uncomfortable with the glass and was worried someone might break a glass and cut me and possibly scar my good looks for life.

"Grandma, would it be possible for me to have a plastic glass?" I asked.

"Tom, we use real glasses on holidays and special occasions. Today is Labor Day, and we celebrate the hard work that men and actually some women now do at the Chrysler factory."

"I would be more comfortable with plastic, but if I have to use a glass, I will."

She looked at me and replied, "I will be happy to get you a plastic cup if you prefer."

I was more comfortable with the plastic cup, but I ate the meal worried about others breaking their glasses. I don't remember being so worried about glass before this time. Maybe hearing about Anna and how she died had heightened my concern about breaking glass.

We had a good meal of corn-on-the-cob along with some Hungarian dishes. After the meal, Rod and I talked more about rock-n-roll. Rod was a big Rolling Stones fan. It was a fun day, but it was time to go home and get ready for my first day of junior high.

— ✦ —

I got up in the morning, put on one of my new outfits and went out to wait for the bus. Since I was now going to junior high school, I caught a different bus than I had the previous year. This school was five miles away instead of one mile away for elementary school. When I got on the bus, I got a seat to myself. To my surprise, the bus stopped near Stan's house, and he got on. He sat in the seat with me, and we talked all the way to school. Stan was no longer a walker for junior high as he had been in elementary school. After several days of getting on the bus, I noticed that everyone boarded the bus and sat in the same seats. This was a much better busing situation than elementary school.

We got to school, and I had to find my homeroom class. Since Stan's last name didn't start with an M like mine, we were in different homerooms. In homeroom, they gave us our schedules. I had French first period, science second period, history third period, math fourth period, English fifth period, choir sixth period and gym seventh period. The only class Stan and I had together was math. It was called Accelerated Math, and it was for the top math students in seventh grade to move faster through the material.

My first day went well, except for history. In history class, there were a couple boys talking near me, and I was listening to what they were saying. Steve and Larry played for the Blue Devils and were talking about how they were better than the Red Devils. I told them I played for the Red Devils.

Just then the teacher looked down at her seating chart, then looked at me and said, "Tom, there's no talking in class."

"I wasn't talking," I replied with a stern look.

"I heard you talking, and you need to pay attention in class."

"I was paying attention," I said, this time a little louder.

"I'm telling you, no more talking." She seemed to be getting a little irritated.

Why did she single me out? Why didn't she say something to the boys who started it? I was hoping for a great year and was disappointed one of my classes had to start like this.

When I got home, I was happy I no longer had to check in with the neighbor lady and had a key to get in my house. I dropped off my books and went down to Gramps' dock. It was quiet there. I sat and thought. Just then, Gramps walked up.

"Tom! How's the All-American doing today?"

"Gramps. Since it's now the fall, I figured you were back at Michigan State."

Gramps laughed. "State is on the quarter system, so I still have two more weeks of enjoying this beautiful lake."

"I really wanted this year to be my year. I wanted to be past any getting in trouble and have a great year in junior high. But first day and already I'm in trouble."

"Oh no! What happened?"

"A couple of the Blue Devils were bragging about beating us in the scrimmage, and I let them know we play them again."

"Good job. The real game will be played at the end of the season."

"The teacher accused me of talking. When I told her I wasn't talking, she got more irritated with me. I just didn't want to get in trouble the first day, and the more I tried to convince her, the worse it got."

"I understand the frustration. Do you want to learn about defensive communication?"

"Defensive communication? Sure."

"Defensiveness is defined as the act of defending ourselves against a personal attack. People say something we don't like, and we feel attacked. It's natural to want to defend or attack back. However, we've talked a lot about goals. Is your goal to show the person communicating to you how stupid their comment was and how wrong they are?"

"She was wrong. She should have said something to those other guys."

"Tom, you told me you talked as well. Avoiding defensive communication is being truthful. Was she wrong that you talked in class?"

"No."

"Our goal should be to be genuine and avoid defensive communication."

"Genuine?"

"Genuine. Real. Truthful."

"In defensive communication, we want to show that we're right and other people are wrong. People don't like to be wrong, so if we make people feel wrong, they won't like us. Did you try to show the teacher she was wrong?"

"I didn't think of it that way at the time. I was just..." I shook my head and laughed a little. "...defending myself."

Gramps laughed a little too. "Now, you told me your goals are to get along with people and get good grades. You also have goals of doing well in sports, having fun and learning new skills."

"I didn't meet my goals today. What do I do when the teacher talks to me this way?"

"You want to be genuine, and you don't want the teacher to feel like you think she's wrong. One option was to do what you did. What's another option?"

"Well, I guess I could have just said, 'yes, ma'am.' Then I would've felt embarrassed that the others in the class would think I'm a trouble maker. I feel like I'd be admitting I started the problem."

"You aren't admitting anything. You're simply complying with the request of someone in authority. In the moment, we want to be impulsive and let the teacher know how stupid she was. In the long run, we want the teacher to like you and for you to get a good grade."

"Yes, that's my goal. I don't want to look like a trouble maker in front of others."

"So, saying 'yes, ma'am' is looking like more of a trouble maker than arguing with the teacher?"

I couldn't help but laugh. Gramps had me again.

"So defensiveness seems like we're defending ourselves against others, but it doesn't work. Defensiveness only helps us defend against feeling uncomfortable."

"Gramps, you've asked me to feel uncomfortable before."

"I have. Yes. The most successful people feel uncomfortable and don't like things, but they behave in the ways they need to achieve long-term goals. Now, if she starts trying to hit you over the head with a baseball bat, defend yourself."

"You're right. This would only be about a three on the 1-to-10-point scale."

I thanked Gramps and headed home. I was determined to work on not being defensive.

On Sunday, we had our first real game of the season and had to travel to Royal Oak to play. Before the game we weighed in, and I again weighed 115 pounds. I'd reminded my mother to try to find the announcers before the game and tell them how to pronounce my name. I can only assume that my mother was uncomfortable with this request and didn't do it, so I was referred to as Moe-China for this game too.

As the game started, Royal Oak scored on their first possession. We had practiced mainly against the run, but this team put the ball in the air a lot. Our offense didn't do very well either. By the time it was my turn to quarterback, we were down 16-0.

I decided to call my own number on the first play and ran the quarterback sneak for 5 yards. I then went to the tailback on the crossbuck play, but we lost 2 yards because their defenders were in our backfield. On third down and 7 yards to go, I tried to run the crossbuck pass, but there were two defensive players on me, and I was only able to push forward for no gain. With the defenders in my face, I couldn't even see who I wanted to throw the ball to. On fourth down, I thought I would be fair and give the ball to the fullback on the dive play to give him a chance to have his name called, but he got stopped for no gain, and we lost the ball on downs.

The second half didn't go much better, and by the time I got my chance to quarterback again, we were down 30-0. I thought about how we could get a first down and decided probably the best strategy was to run the quarterback sneak every play and try to get four or five yards each time. Although this might have worked, I didn't think the other players or the parents would be happy with this play calling.

I decided to open up with the option. I faked the ball to the fullback on the dive and came down the line only to come face to face with a defensive player, so I faked a pitch. He followed the fake, and I took off running. After three guys had tried to bring me down, I fell forward for a gain of 12 yards and a first down. Although the result of this play was me running the ball like a quarterback sneak, I don't think it looked as selfish.

Neither my offense nor the first-team offense had much luck with the crossbuck runs. I decided to run the crossbuck pass to the left, knowing I would have to pass the ball more quickly than I'd practiced. I gave the fakes and saw the tight end open, so I threw to him, but he couldn't hold on for the catch. I decided to run the same play to right and tried the same throw to the tight end on the right side. He caught the ball for a gain of 5 yards.

It was third and 5, so I decided to call for the quarterback sneak and pushed forward for another first down. As we got back in the huddle, the first-team offense ran onto the field and my four plays for that half came to end. I ran off the field and didn't even look at Coach Patterson, but he called for me to come over.

"Tom, you looked really good out there. I know you're disappointed about your playing time at quarterback, but I want you to keep playing the way you did today. I do notice how well you're playing. This was a tough game for all of us."

"Thanks, Coach."

I walked away. The coach was right. I was disappointed in my playing time. But I was happy he liked my play. I had two options: I could complain about my playing time, or I could keep trying to earn more. This was a tough choice for a 12-year-old kid.

Mademoiselle

O n Monday morning, I caught the bus and arrived at school. The day went fairly well without any problems. I'd always enjoyed singing and was excited to be in the seventh grade boys' choir, which met sixth period.

During the first week of school, we just sang some fun songs and the instructor, Mr. Jett, asked each of us to sing for him individually to assess which group we would be placed in. There were four groups which created the four-part harmony: first tenor, second tenor, baritone, and bass. The choir room had tiered seating so he could see everyone. He asked that the first tenors sit in the first row, the second tenors in the second row, the baritones in the third row and the basses up top on the fourth row.

He called all of our names and told us what part we would be singing. Most of the bigger guys who played football were in the back two rows and the smaller guys in the first two rows. I was a bigger guy who played football, but I ended up in the front row with the first tenors.

That day, we didn't sing any music that required parts. We sang some fun songs which included "John Jacob Jingleheimer Schmidt" and "Kookaburra":

Kookaburra sits in the old gum tree. Merry king of the bush is he. Laugh kookaburra, laugh kookaburra, fun your life must be.

We didn't know it at the time, but Mr. Jett took liberties with changing some lyrics. We just assumed that the lyrics he gave us were the lyrics. However, I found out years later he'd substituted the word *fun* for *gay* because *gay* was just starting to be used as a term for homosexual.

After class, I asked Mr. Jett if I was in the right group because the taller boys seemed to be in the back, and I was much taller than anyone in the front row.

"Tom, height actually has nothing to do with how I separated the group. When you were being tested, you sang very well on the high notes and struggled a little with the lower notes. I'm thinking you will be one of my star tenors. John Lennon and Paul McCartney are outstanding tenors. Do you ever sing along with them?"

"Of course. The Beatles are great."

"I know it might be embarrassing for you to be in the front row, but you're there because I see some talent in you. I hope this will be okay?"

"Thanks, Mr. Jett. I'll do my best."

On Tuesday, my French teacher let the class go to the library. I saw a group of girls all laughing and talking about something. All three were walkers to the junior high school, so they'd attended Union Lake Elementary School. Melanie was attractive but a little overweight. Kay was attractive but had some complexion problems.

Kate was very attractive and very thin with long brown hair and green eyes. All were dressed very well. They were varsity cheerleaders for the Blue Devils. Kay and Melanie seemed more outgoing than Kate.

Hearing the girls laughing, I couldn't help but look at them. Then Kay said, "*Bonjour*, Tom. *Comment ça va?*"

"*Trés bien*, but what is so funny?" I asked, using the little French I'd learned in class.

"Kate is grossed out by this book."

"Why? What's wrong with it?"

"It's too gross. We can't show you."

Of course, this made me want to see it even more. Was it naked people? What could it be? "Come on, let's see."

"Keep that book away from me. Yuck!" exclaimed Kate.

Kay opened the book, and I looked intensely. There were a lot of words and one small picture on each page. One picture showed a fence and a house. The other looked like a field. I couldn't figure it out. What was I missing?

"Ew, isn't it sick?" said Kate.

I looked at Melanie. "I don't get it."

The girls laughed. "You don't see it?" said Melanie.

Kay pointed to a spot on the page that just looked like dirt to me at first. Then I figured it out. It was a booger! Someone had picked their nose and left it in the book. It didn't really faze me that much, but I was there with three popular, good-looking girls, so I said, "Oh, that is sick." I squinted my eyes and turned up my nose. "*Au revoir*, ladies."

"*Au revoir*," they each said and went back to laughing.

On Wednesday after French class, Kay and Melanie started walking with me, smiling. I looked at them.

Kay said, "Kate likes you and wants to be your girlfriend."

I looked around to see who may have heard this. My eyebrows raised in almost disbelief.

"Just wanted to tell you in case you want a girlfriend," she added.

This was one of those times when it was so hard to know what to say. In my opinion, Kate was one of the best-looking girls in the seventh grade. I just said, "Wow, thank you."

"See ya, Tommy," said Melanie.

"Bye, Tommy," added Kay, smiling from ear to ear.

Not many people call me Tommy, but I could tell they were having fun teasing me. However, I'd been given some information and tried to decide what I should do with it. I knew I couldn't wait too long or Kate might take it as rejection.

On Thursday, I walked into French class and looked for Kate. I looked at her, but she didn't look back. Should I say hello or not say anything? I felt embarrassed so I just sat down. I could hear the girls laughing.

"*Bonjour, classe*," said Ms. Carter.

"*Bonjour, Mademoiselle Carter*," we all responded in unison.

I participated in class but was distracted thinking about Kate. When the bell rang, I walked out into the hall. The three girls walked out, and I started following them. I heard Kay say, "Melanie and I have to go back to the choir room. See you later, Kate." They both looked at me and smiled really big.

I walked up to Kate and tried to start a conversation. "How'd you like French today?"

"Oh, it was okay."

"I hope you haven't found any more gross things in books."

"Ew! No, not today," Kate said, turning her nose up.

I was getting closer to my next class, so I said, "Nice talking to you, Kate."

"Bye," was her only response.

I was proud of myself for trying to talk with Kate given the information that she wanted to be my girlfriend but trying to talk to her was like pulling teeth. She was as good looking as Teresa, but just not as talkative. I decided I would keep trying, because I would gain tremendous status at this school if people started to think she was my girlfriend.

On Friday, I walked with her after French class again. We exchanges greetings, and she smiled at me. It seemed like she liked me. "What class do you have next hour?"

"English, yuck," she responded.

That was our conversation for the day. I wish I'd asked her something to get a more positive response. I really struggled trying to make conversation with her. That evening after football practice, I headed down to look for Gramps. Luckily he was outside, so I told him about Kate.

"Tommy Boy, I wish I was your age again with your looks. You land all of the great-looking ladies."

"I just don't know what to say to her."

"It sounds like she's shy. Maybe you're already saying the right things."

"Maybe, but when I try to talk to her, she usually responds with the word *yuck*."

"How does she respond when you kiss her? Gramps said with a smile.

I just laughed.

"Tom, it seems like you might be forcing things a little. Just be yourself. Hopefully, she'll like you for you. Be genuine with her. Tell her about playing football. Ask her about cheerleading."

On Saturday, a new show debuted on television that created a lot of controversy. All of the shows up until now featured married couples with the husband working and the mother usually staying home with the children. The new show was called *Mary Tyler Moore* and featured Mary Tyler Moore as a single working woman. I was excited to see it.

It seemed like my mother was one of the few mothers who held a full-time job. She was planning on watching the show too. Lucky for me, Vito did not come over that night, so my mother and I enjoyed the show together.

On Sunday, we had our second straight away game. This game was in Farmington against a team called Farmington Green. Farmington had two teams too, so they called their teams Green and Blue. Farmington teams had a reputation for being very good.

The Farmington game didn't go a whole lot better than the Royal Oak game. Our offense struggled and didn't score any points. I tried to run some crossbuck plays when I played quarterback, and none of them worked. I carried the ball twice myself for a total of 6 yards and didn't get any passes off. We lost the game 20-0.

Maybe the only good part about the day was that the announcers actually pronounced my name correctly. I asked my mother after the game if she had talked to the announcers, but she said no. I could only assume I got lucky with the Farmington announcers.

When we got home, my mother wanted to rake leaves, so I helped her. We each had a rake. We started in the front yard and raked all of the leaves toward the woods and then into the woods. After we'd finished the front yard, we went and worked on the back yard. My mother wanted the leaves raked into a big pile.

"Mom, can I jump in the pile?"

My mother smiled and said, "of course."

"Let me get my football."

I came out with my football, ran toward the pile of leaves and jumped up and into the pile. "Mom, don't I look just like Steve Owens, the rookie running back of the Detroit Lions?"

"You look just like him," my mother said with smile.

I'm sure she hadn't heard of him. I continued to jump in the pile a few more times and then I asked my mother if she wanted me to rake the leaves into the woods.

"No, Tom. Let's burn them."

We raked the leaves up into a tight pile. My mother got the hose out, just in case the fire got out of control, and then she asked me if I wanted to light them.

"Wow! That would be great!"

It took me few times to get the match to light, but when I did, I was able to start the leaves burning. My mother and I watched them burn.

"How is school going?"

"It's going well. I'm doing really well in accelerated math. I got a 100 on the first quiz. I think I'm doing well in the other classes too. I really enjoy *le classe de français*."

"French class?"

I smiled. "Yes, French. I also really like choir. Mr. Jett thinks I have some talent, but I'm concerned that he wants me to sing the high notes."

"Your father had a high voice for a man. I hope you don't mind this. Your father is a very good singer, but I couldn't ever get him to sing for me."

"It's a little embarrassing, but I'll be fine."

"Any trouble with other boys?"

"No, Mom. I seem to be doing better controlling my anger and getting along with others."

"Tom, I'm so proud of you."

We waited until the leaves burned up and then we hosed down the ashes.

"Though it worries me to say,
I've never felt this way..
I don't know what I'm up against.
I don't know what it's all about.
I got so much to think about."
— The Partridge Family (1970)

Pushing Buttons

On Monday morning after homeroom, I went over to French class. I saw Kate sitting there and smiled at her. She smiled but didn't say anything. I sat down as class started, and I enjoyed the challenge of trying to learn French. After class, I waited for Kate to walk with her.

"Hi, did you have a good weekend?" I asked.
"It was okay."
"How did cheerleading go on Sunday?"
"It was fine. We lost to Farmington Blue."
"We lost to Farmington Green."
She didn't really say anything else, so we just kept walking. A lot of students looked at us and must have assumed we were together. A lot of guys thought Kate was attractive, so I was becoming more popular by being around her than anything else I seemed to do. As she got close to her next class we just exchanged byes and I kept going to my science class.

An hour later in history class, the guys from the Blue Devils wanted to know how we did in our game. I started to tell them and the teacher said, "Tom, no talking."

Since I'd talked to Gramps about this, I was able to respond better. "Yes ma'am." That ended the conversation, and this response seemed to go a lot better than trying to argue with her.

The class that students had fourth period determined the time we went to lunch. I had the accelerated math class fourth period with Stan, so Stan and I would go to lunch together and look for some of the other baseball or football players to sit with. Denny and Floyd spotted us and sat down. Both were back-row basses in choir and both were playing on the junior high football team, probably because they were over the 120-pound weight limit.

"Hey, Tom. You cool?" Floyd said, making his voice even deeper than it already was.

"Hey, Tom," Denny said, purposely making his voice much higher than it normally was.

I knew they were trying to have fun with me for being in the front row in choir, so I played along.

"Floyd, Denny, yes, you guys are the men because you're basses and on the school football team. You guys know, Stan?"

"Stan The Man, from baseball fame! I've heard you're some kind of good baseball player!" said Denny.

"Next year, we'll all be together on the school team for football," responded Stan.

"I'm hip. Can't wait. It's tough getting any kind of playing time as seventh graders," said Floyd.

"Tom,   actually *you* are the man! Kate is some kind of hot chick. What's it like to be kissing her?" said Denny.

84

"Wouldn't you guys want to know? I can't reveal any private intimate information."

"What? Come on, man! Let us live through you!"

We all started laughing. I didn't really want the guys to know that not had I not kissed her or held her hand, I could barely get her to talk.

That Monday evening was another special day for television. It was the first NFL Monday Night Football game ever. I was excited to watch it. It was fun listening to Howard Cosell badger with Dandy Don. The halftime was great because they showed highlights of the Sunday games. Besides the local team, the Detroit Lions, we didn't get a lot of coverage of the other teams. And I didn't get to watch the Lions because our team, the Red Devils, played at the same time, but it was fun watching the highlights of their 40-0 win over the Green Bay Packers. I just knew the Lions would go all the way to the Super Bowl this year.

On Tuesday in history class, the guys from the Blue Devils started in on me.

"You're the quarterback and your team hasn't even scored a point yet. Maybe they need to put you at guard and get a new quarterback," said Steve, one of the Blue Devils.

"Why don't you just shut up until we play? You guys haven't won any more games than we have."

"Hey, at least we've scored a few points!"

I got a little louder. "Just keep your mouth shut until we play."

The teacher looked over at me sternly. She didn't have to say anything. She could tell I wasn't pleased. It was hard for me to concentrate during this class. I just kept quiet.

The next day, Steve started in on me again before class. "Still playing quarterback or did you get demoted?" I didn't even look at him. "Must have been demoted."

"What's wrong with you? Why don't you mind your own business?"

Class started, and I'm sure the teacher could tell I was irritated again. After class she asked me if everything was okay.

"Everything is good except I wish there was an accelerated history class so I didn't have to be in here with retards."

"All seventh graders take the same history class."

"I know. Thank you, ma'am." I walked out and on to my next class.

After football practice, while my mother started cooking dinner, I walked down to look for Gramps. He was out on his deck relaxing. He invited me to join him on the deck.

"Gramps, I'm having a little difficulty in history class."

"Tom, you're one of the smartest kids I know. What's the trouble?"

"Thanks. It's not the school work. It is a couple guys who push my buttons."

"Push your buttons?"

"You know, they purposely irritate me."

"Where are your buttons? You have buttons and anyone can push them to change your mood?"

"Yes, doesn't everyone have buttons? What if someone called you a bad doctor? That would push your buttons."

"Let's try it. Call me a bad doctor."

"Gramps, I can't say that."

"Fair enough, Tom, but many people have called me a bad doctor."

"What?   You?"

"People come in to my office with expectations about what they want. If I determine they need something different, they sometimes call me a bad doctor or even worse. But I don't let it bother me, even though I don't like it. I don't wear buttons, so no one can push them. Tom, if you take off your coat of buttons, no one can push them."

"How do I do that?"

"It's a mindset. You have to remember you won't be liked by everyone. If 70 percent of the people like you, you're doing well. You have to expect 30 percent of the people to say rude things, and if you're not wearing the coat of buttons, they will have nothing to push. If you allow people to push your buttons, you're allowing jerks to control you."

"All right, Gramps. I'll take off my coat of buttons and see how it goes. I'll expect Steve to act like a jerk, but he's not going to control me. Thanks."

Just then Mrs. Davis came out. I don't see her that often. "Tom, I baked all of these cookies. Would you please take them home and share them with your mother?"

"Thanks, Mrs. Davis."

"You're welcome, Tom," she replied as she went back in the house.

"Hey, Gramps, I've got a couple new friends. They're two of the bigger guys in seventh grade who play on the junior high team. They're from Dublin Elementary. I met them through the choir, and now they eat lunch with Stan and me. Hopefully we'll all be teammates on the school team next year."

"Good. I'm glad you're looking forward to next year. It looks like the school team next year will be a good mix of those on the team this year, the Red Devils and the Blue Devils."

I breathed out a minute. "Blue Devils. I hadn't really thought about them being my teammates."

"If you all play high school football, those guys could be your teammates for the next five years!"

"Five years? That sounds like forever! How can I be friends with those guys?"

"I would try to understand, accept and appreciate. So first, understand what they're trying to tell you. Are they trying to have fun with you because you have an important position of quarterback, or are they just trying to be hurtful? Accept them for them. In elementary school, you mainly went to school with children of the working class, but in junior high, those from Union Lake Elementary mainly come from professional families. They grew up a little differently. Their parents were able to get the junior high school built in their backyard."

"So accept them for who they are?"

"Yes, and accept that they may think differently than you."

"Is Dublin a rich area?"

"I think Dublin is more like Twin Beach."

"Floyd and Denny are from Dublin, but...Kate is from Union Lake Elementary." I pondered this for a moment.

"You may have some tighter bonds with the Twin Beach and Dublin kids, but you have to get along with people from all of the schools, including Union Lake."

"So accept them for them?"

"Yes. Third step. Appreciate them. Try to find the good in them. If they win a game, congratulate them."

"I'll try. Thanks. We have our first home game this Sunday."

"Share those cookies with your mother. You need to make the weight for this year."

The rest of the week went fairly well. I still walked Kate to class, but she had little to say. I didn't hear much from Steve in history class. Choir was still fun. The highlight of every day at school became the joking around with Floyd, Denny, and Stan at lunch.

That Friday night another new show was coming out. It was called *The Partridge Family* and starred the musical group of the same name. Being a music fan, I quickly made this show one of my favorites.

On Sunday, my mother took me to the Walled Lake Western field for our first home game. I arrived and chatted with Stan and the other players, and then the coach asked us to line up for weigh-in. When it was my turn, the scale read 119 pounds.

"Tom, you better lay off the desserts or you won't be playing in future games."

"Oh, I will." The bag of cookies Mrs. Davis had given me were great. I liked them so much, I ate them all. This was a dilemma. I had to give up desserts to play football. This would be very hard.

Farmington Blue had to kick off to us first. Kevin's first-team offense ran four crossbucks and got enough for a first down but then ran another four plays and were stopped, so I got on the field for the first time that game on defense. After two running plays, they tried an option my way, and I was able to tackle the quarterback for a 1-yard loss.

"Williams, the ball carrier, brought down for a 1-yard loss by Moe-China."

I couldn't believe it. My mother hadn't talked to the people announcing the game. *How am I ever going to be famous if they don't know my name?*

We made it through the first quarter with no one scoring, and I was ready for my four plays at quarterback in the second quarter. I'd been watching the defense and saw that they played two tackles and no nose guard, so I tried the quarterback sneak on first down. I got through the line, and they hit me after a gain of 2 yards. I was able to drag them for 2 more yards and fall forward for 2 more yards.

"Mochina, the ball carrier, brought down by a host of Farmington Blues after a gain of 6 yards."

They pronounced my name correctly! That was more exciting than gaining the 6 yards. Did my mother actually go tell them?

I wanted to run the crossbuck next, so I ran it at 6 to give to the fullback. Hopefully he wouldn't lose yardage. The play worked for 2 yards. I then went to the crossbuck at 3 to give the tailback a chance, and he gained 3 yards for a first down. I had one more play. I thought about making it a big one, but the crossbucks were working, so I went back to the crossbuck at 6 and our fullback gained 3 more yards.

After the play, the first team came running on to the field and I had to leave. I knew I only had four plays, so as I ran to the sidelines this time, I wasn't disappointed. I was happy we'd been able to move the ball. The coach was clapping as we came off the field.

I looked up to find my mother in the stands and noticed Charlie, Gramps' son, and his wife sitting near her. Maybe it was Charlie who went up to tell them how to pronounce my name. I was happy he was here to watch. The half ended in a 0-0 tie. We had a good chance to win our first game, and how sweet it would be with Charlie in the stands.

The game remained scoreless as the fourth quarter started and I came on to the field to run my four plays. We had good field position with the ball on the other team's 49 yard line. I felt now was the time to win this game, and running the ball up with middle wasn't going to be enough. I called an option pass on the first play. As I ran out to try to throw the ball, there was a defender right on me. I went to pitch the ball, and he hit my arm. The ball bounced to the tailback who fell on it for a loss of 6 yards.

The next two plays, I tried the crossbuck passes, and both times I had to hurry my throws because of pressure from the defense. Both were incomplete passes. It was now fourth down and 16 yards to go. I decided to go back to the option and make a quicker throw or pitch. As I came down the line, the defender came up to me, and I pitched the ball to the tailback, who got tackled for no gain.

I'd come in wanting to be the star, and we ended up losing 6 yards and giving Farmington the ball on our 45 yard line. It only took three plays for them to score. On the third play, they ran a trap play up the middle, and their tailback ran 38 yards for a touchdown.

We ended up losing 8-0, but the worst part was that I played a key role in the defeat. Why didn't I stay with the running game that had worked in the first half? Maybe I would've given the ball to our first-team offense with only 35 yards to go and *they* would've scored the only touchdown.

I came off the field and found Charlie standing there. He knew I was disappointed. He looked at me and said, "Tom, I'm so proud of how well you played."

"Thanks, Charlie."

> *"Ground control to Major Tom.*
> *Ground control to Major Tom.*
> *Take your protein pills and put your helmet on.*
> *Ground control to Major Tom."*
> — *David Bowie (1969)*

Second Half

On Monday morning, I got to history class and was expecting to be harassed by Steve and Larry about another scoreless game, but before they got a chance to say anything, I asked how their game went.

"That Farmington Green team is tough. We lost big. How'd you guys do?" asked Larry.

"We lost, and yes, you guessed it, we still haven't scored a point. I guess we're saving all of our points for the Blue Devil game," I said and then laughed.

"We don't want that. You guys better score this week."

We sat down and began the lesson. I thought about what Gramps had said about these guys being my future teammates and knew I would do better to accept them for being them. I knew they would harass me and why not? We're stinking up the league. If I want praise when we do well, I have to be able to take the crap when we perform poorly.

In French class, I noticed Kate wasn't there. After class, I walked with Kay and Melanie, who were smiling as always.

"When are you going to hold hands with Kate? If you don't like her, you can hold my hand, Tommy," said Kay, smiling from ear to ear.

"Hold her hand? I can't get two words out of her. I don't think she likes me."

"She does. She tells me. And I tell her if she doesn't hurry up and hold your hand, then I'll take you from her."

There was no doubt that Kate was very good looking, but Kay was much more fun.

"Where is Kate today?"

"Oh, she's sick. She's got a cold."

"Well, I'm not going to hold her hand if she's sick."

After school and football practice, I went down to the lake to look for Gramps, but didn't see him out. I sat on the log that separated the beach area from the grass area and looked out over the water. After about 10 minutes, I could hear Mrs. Davis calling my name from the deck. I walked closer to her.

"Tom, Gramps is back teaching at Michigan State and won't be here much in the evenings. He told me that if I see you to tell you to come and say hi to him on the weekends."

"Okay."

"Do you want some more cookies?"

"I really enjoyed the cookies, but I better not take any more. I was only one pound away from not making weight for football. As soon as the football season is over, I would love to have some."

I headed back home for the evening and had some ring bologna and "make believe" potatoes. My mother called them "make believe" because they were potato flakes that came in a box.

She turned them into mashed potatoes by adding boiling water and butter.

In choir we started learning "The Man on Flying Trapeze." For the refrain, the baritones sang the melody. The tenors sang the "poo, poo," and Mr. Jett had us leaning and bobbing our heads each time we sang "poo." The basses sang "poo" as low notes and squatted when they sang. It was funny to see the basses squat each "poo." The end result of everyone together sounded like a pipe organ with the low "poo" followed by the high "poo, poo." There was also a low solo for the basses, and Floyd got to sing it by himself. I would try to sing it at home.

"The girl that I love she is handsome to see.
I tried all I knew her to please."

It was a real stretch for me to sing that low.

I woke up Saturday only to see on the front page of the newspaper that the Wichita State football team had been in an airplane crash and most of the team had died. Wow! These guys made it all the way to college football and got to fly on an airplane like the pros and this happened. I couldn't think about anything else. I'd never been on an airplane. I started fearing airplanes.

After lunch, I headed down to the lake. Gramps and Charlie were sitting on the deck.

"Hey, Tom. Come on over," I heard Charlie say.

"Charlie, did you straighten out that announcer about my last name?"

Charlie laughed. "It wasn't me, but I know who it was."

"Who? Not my mother?"

"No. It was Stan's dad. After they first announced you incorrectly, he made a dash to the press box. He came back and told us he'd told them how to pronounce your name, and if they couldn't remember it to just call you The Machine."

"I'll have to thank Coach next time I see him. Did you hear about the plane crash?"

"Awful. Terrible. I can't even imagine," said Charlie.

"Well, you got to watch our stinky football team. Maybe I better stick to baseball."

"Hey, you looked good. You play solid on the defensive end and looked good at quarterback. Your defense played well. For almost the entire game, you played what I call 'bend but don't break'."

"Thanks. However, we broke at the end."

"That other coach called a good play. He split the receivers and forced your defensive backs out wide. Then the trap block worked and there was no one to run down the ball carrier."

Most football fans probably only saw the guy with the ball. Charlie knew football. He was able to see the entire field.

When I got home, my mother told me she was going out with Vito to see the new movie *M.A.S.H.* She made me a tuna fish sandwich with chicken noodle soup. I told her to have fun and that I would be fine at home alone.

I heard a knock at the door and knew who it was, so I decided to go to my bedroom and not see him. I didn't want him to ask me about the game last week or have to hear how well his kids did. I was able to stay in the bedroom until they left.

I turned on my favorite 45 records and sang along. I also sang some of the choir stuff. It was a great time to sing and no one else would hear.

— ◆ —

The next day was another home game against one of the Waterford teams. Again I prepared myself to play well on defense and do the best I could on my eight plays on offense. I played fairly well on defense, but we got down 6-0 in the first quarter. I was still happy that the announcer was pronouncing my name correctly.

To start the second quarter, I got my four plays at quarterback and ran four crossbucks, giving twice to the fullback and twice to the tailback. We only gained 6 yards and gave the ball up on downs.

Late in the second half we were down 12-0. Kevin called an option play to the left, and he got hit hard by two players and fumbled the ball. The Bears recovered it. I was ready to run back on the field to play defense, but Kevin was not getting off the ground. The coaches ran out on the field and stood over him. After several minutes, they got Kevin to his feet and helped him walk off the field.

"Defense, let's go!" roared Coach Patterson.

I ran on to the field and played my right defensive end position for two more plays until the clock ran out for halftime.

At halftime, we all sat under one of the goal posts to rest. All of a sudden, I heard Coach Patterson say, "Tom Mochina."

I got up and trotted over to talk to him.

"I'm not going to play Kevin in the second half. Can you go all the way at quarterback and also play defense?"

"Coach, of course. I'm ready."

"I saw you were conservative in the play calling in the first half. I want you to mix it up. Run the ball yourself some. They'll have a hard time tackling you."

I looked at the coach and just repeated, "I'm ready."

We got the ball first in the second half at our own 36 yard line. I decided to try the quarterback sneak on the first play, and it must have surprised them because I gained 14 yards to midfield. On the second play, I ran the crossbuck to the tailback, and he gained 6 yards.

I got back to the huddle and was thinking we only needed 4 yards and could run the ball up the middle again. Then I looked at Stan and realized that this was the first time we'd played offense together. Since Stan was playing wingback, I called the crossbuck pass. Even if it didn't work and the ball fell incomplete, I felt I could run the ball myself on third down and get the first down.

I faked to the fullback, then faked to the tailback and sprinted out like I was going to run. Then I slowed up a little and threw the ball to Stan, who caught the ball and headed up field. One defender dove at his feet but didn't touch him. The rest of the defenders chased Stan into the end zone but couldn't catch him.

Stan had scored our first touchdown of the season! He came back to the huddle because we still had to try our two-point conversion not having someone to kick extra points. He looked at me, and I nodded to him. There weren't any high fives or chest bumps. We had our next challenge of the extra point. I decided to run the crossbuck to the tailback, but they were ready for it, and we didn't get the extra point.

I headed off the field for the kickoff. Stan stayed on because he was on the kickoff team. Coach Patterson was all smiles.

"Tom, way to go! Keep it up!"

The Waterford Bears got the ball, and they started driving down the field. We finally stopped them at our own 22 yard line.

I ran a couple crossbucks for a total of 5 yards, and then I tried the option play. I kept the ball myself and gained 5 yards for the first down. I then ran the option the other way but pitched it this time, and our tailback gained 12 yards. Next up was the crossbuck pass. This time, I threw the ball a little low. Stan was able to catch it, but he only got 8 yards. A quarterback sneak got us 6 more yards and a first down.

I ran a couple more crossbucks for a total of 4 yards. I then tried the sneak, but I only got 3 yards. It was fourth down. I thought my best chance to get the first down was to sneak it again and not let them get me down until I had at least 4 yards. I ran the play, and they hit me after about a 1-yard gain, but I refused to go down. I kept moving forward and finally fell for a 4-yard gain.

On first down at the Bears' 45 yard line, I went back to the crossbuck pass. Stan caught the ball on the run, but they pushed him out of bounds after a gain of 25 yards. On the next three plays, the fullback, the tailback and I ran the ball once each and gained 11 yards to the 9 yard line. I then tried the option play, and as they came to tackle me, I pitched the ball to the tailback who ran 9 yards for the touchdown.

The score was now tied, and we needed to get the extra point to break the tie. I remembered how they were jammed in tight on the last extra point attempt, so I decided to run the same option play that we'd just scored on. Again the defense came to me, and I pitched the ball to the tailback for the two points. We led 14-12. This time many of the players were jumping up and down, but I just hustled back to the sidelines.

"Let's be tough on defense now," Coach Patterson yelled.

The Bears started out running the ball and were gaining first downs. We were bending but not breaking. With only a minute left, the Bears ran a play action pass, and we were all trying so hard to stop the run that a receiver got open down field. Their quarterback threw him a pass, and we were not able to catch him. They added a two-point conversion and they now led 20-12.

They kicked off to us. I had 45 seconds. Coach Patterson came up to me and said, "Tom, all passes. If you run the ball, the clock will keep running. Just tell them in the huddle that every play will crossbuck pass at 7 on one. There will be no more huddles. Just get them up to the line and keep running the play.

We got on the field, and I told the team what we were going to do. We hadn't ever practiced this, but now we had to perform. On the first play, I was able to throw the ball to Stan for 20 yards, and he was able to get out of bounds to stop the clock. We lined up again, but this time Stan was covered so I threw the ball to our tight end for 8 yards, but he didn't get out of bounds. The clock was running.

We lined up as quickly as we could, and I tried to throw the ball to Stan again, but we didn't connect. It was now third down with only 9 seconds left. We lined up, and I threw the ball out to Stan who caught it, but a defensive player dove at his feet and got him down in bounds. We were not able to get another play off and lost the game.

After the game, the coach said, "Don't feel bad. You did well. We won the second half for the first time all year. You just ran out of time. If we'd had three or four more minutes, I think we would have won."

After the game, Charlie was waiting for me. Again, I probably didn't look that happy because we lost. "Tom, wow—you really played well. So close. That was an enjoyable second half."

Defensive End

"I never thought I could feel this way.
And I've got to say that I just don't get it.
I don't know where we went wrong,
But the feeling's gone and I just can't get it back."
— *Gordon Lightfoot (1970)*

Hot Chow

After the game I just relaxed and watched television. The big news story of the day was that rock star Janis Joplin had died of an apparent drug overdose. A few weeks earlier it had been reported that rock star Jimi Hendrix had also died of a drug overdose. These were two very famous people. Neither of whom got to live to see their 28th birthday. I still dreamed of being a famous rock star, but I was determined to be a drug-free lead singer. I was sad about the deaths. This was just more evidence for me that I never wanted to do drugs.

On Monday, I got to history early to wait for Steve's question about we had scored a touchdown yet, and he didn't disappoint me.

"You guys still scoreless?"

"Nope. We scored 14 points."

"Man, the Red Devils are moving up. I'm scared. Did your other quarterback score your points?"

"Wrong again. I threw a touchdown pass to Stan for the first score. I helped drive the team down for a second score running and passing, and our tailback scored the touchdown and extra point. How many touchdowns did you score?"

"We had a rough game and lost 20-6. I didn't score the touchdown."

"Quiet, please!" the teacher said as class started. I guessed the best way to stop the criticizing was to tell Steve about some success.

The next hour was science class, which was taught by Mr. Edgerton. The joke in this class was that some of the boys said something as they sneezed. One boy last week sneezed the teacher's name, and another sneezed *day off*. I'm not sure why I found this so amusing, but I laughed a little inside every time. I'm also not sure why I chose this day, but I decided to give it a try when I felt a sneeze coming on. Instead of saying *ah choo*, I sneezed *hot chow*. The class started laughing.

"Tom, it's only second period, and you're hungry already," said Mr. Edgerton.

I felt really embarrassed, but I could see Mr. Edgerton smile so I survived this embarrassing moment. I never sneezed anything again in his class, but outside of class, *hot chow* became my go-to sneeze.

At lunch, Stan and I walked up to sit with Denny and Floyd.

Denny said in a very high voice, "Hi, Tom."

I started laughing and said in my lowest voice, "Denny."

"Man, Stan you look a lot better. I just can't figure out what it is," said Floyd.

"My parents made me get a haircut," Stan replied.

"I'm hip. You look a lot hipper than Joe Namath over there," Floyd said, pointing to me.

My hair was getting longer. In this case it may have been an advantage not to have a father at home to make me get my hair cut. My mother didn't want to go through the trouble of trying to drag me to get this done, but I knew she didn't like it.

"Yeah, Joe Namath. I was thinking Keith Partridge, but I'll go with a quarterback." Keith Partridge was the stage name of David Cassidy of the Partridge family.

We talked about the game. Denny and Floyd weren't getting a lot of playing time on the school team. It was fun that I got to talk with Stan about our touchdown.

After school, we went to football practice. Coach Patterson told me he wanted me to run plays with the first-team offense because Kevin was still recovering from his injury. I was happy to do this. I watched Kevin run plays with the second team, and he looked fine. I was being given an opportunity, like Gramps had talked about. It was now my job to make the most of it. I worked really hard.

The coach put in two new plays, and we also worked on the reverse to the wingback, which I hadn't run yet. The first new play was called the tight end quickie. In this play, the tight ends ran a quick slant toward the middle, and I got the ball to whoever was the most open. The other play we put in was called the power sweep. On this one, there were no fakes. I pitched to the tailback, and we all led the blocking—including me. We continued to work on these plays all week, as well as our normal offense.

The Lions played in the Monday Night Football game that night at Tiger Stadium. Back in 1970, they turned a baseball park into a football field for the Lions home games. I was excited about the game, but the Lions trailed 7-0 at halftime. I wanted the Lions to play quarterback

Greg Landry, but they stayed with Bill Munson for the entire game. In the second half, Mel Farr ran for two touchdowns and my Lions won! They were now 3-0. Since the Vikings had just lost to Green Bay, I was looking forward to the visit from Vito this week.

On Wednesday, I went to French class. We had already learned the phrase, *do you have a friend in French class?* with the responses of both *Yes, I have a friend in French class* and *No, I don't have a friend in French class*. The tricky part to this was noticing if the teacher said *un* for a male friend or *une* for a female friend. Now we were learning *What is his or her name?* and *His or her name is Tom,* or whoever you chose.

The teacher looked me and asked, "*Avéz-vous une amie dans la classe de français?*"

I had to think quickly. She said *une*. So I knew my response. "*Oui. J'ai une amie dans la classe de français.*"

"*Comment s'appelle t'elle?*" The teacher asked me to tell her name.

"*Elle s'appelle Kate.*"

"Ah," said the teacher, smiling. Then she looked at Kate and asked her if she had a male friend in French class. Kate responded that she did. The teacher then asked, "*Comment s'appelle t'il?*"

Kate responded, "*Il s'appelle David.*"

David? What? I didn't even look at her. Why would she say that? I wasn't afraid to say her name. Why didn't she say mine? This was the last straw. I'd tried to get to know her and walk with her, and then she pulled this? After class I just got up and left. I didn't wait to walk with her.

The next day Kay caught me after class.
"Why didn't you walk with Kate?"

"I assumed she wanted to walk with David."

"She likes you, but she was embarrassed to
say it in class."

"Well, I want someone who isn't
embarrassed by me."

I never really talked to Kate again that year.
I was sad about it for several days. Maybe if she
was fun and we'd talked, I could have gotten over
the David comment, but there weren't enough
positives to overcome this negative.

On Thursday night, while I was watching
TV I heard my mother talking on the phone. I
heard her say she was going out with Vito on
Friday. Since we lived in such a small house, it was
easy to hear anything she said on the phone. Then
I heard her say he was planning on leaving his
wife, but he had to wait to explain it to his
children. What? Vito was married! This was the
first I had heard this. Why would my mother want
to date a married man? Since I already didn't like
him, this added some fuel to the fire.

When my mother got off the phone I asked
her. "Is Vito married?"

"Tom, Vito is my friend. We enjoy spending
time together."

"Is he married?" I asked again.

"He's separated. He lives in the basement,
and his wife and children live on the main floor."

"How do you know? Have you been to his
house? Does his wife know you are, um, friends?"

"I have not been to his house and have not
met his wife. He said he will get divorced when he
can, and I trust him."

On Friday night, Vito came over, and this time I decided to stay out in the living room.

"Hey, Vito, did you see the Lions game Monday?"

"Yes, they can beat the Bears, but they won't beat the Vikings."

"I saw the Packers just beat the Vikings, and the Lions creamed the Packers."

He greeted my mother, and she got her coat.

"Tom, I'll be back soon."

"Okay, Mom, I'm going to watch the Partridge Family. Have fun getting some hot chow!"

Vito hadn't bragged about his kids this week, and he hadn't said anything about me doing well at quarterback, even though I'd heard my mother telling him about my football game on the phone earlier in the week.

On Saturday, I headed to the lake, and Gramps was out.

"Tom Mochina, star quarterback," he said as I walked up. "I bet a star quarterback doesn't help move picnic tables."

"I'll be happy to help you with whatever you want," I told him with a smile.

"The boats are up on shore for the winter. I just need a little help with the picnic table."

While I helped him, he told me he'd talked to Charlie and heard I'd played quarterback well.

"Gramps, I practiced with the first team this week, so I think I'm starting tomorrow. I had an opportunity last week, and I did well. I have an opportunity tomorrow, and I'm going to try my best." We kept working, and I told Gramps I'd been doing better with not being so defensive.

"To not be defensive, we have to be accountable for our own actions. When you lose a game or things don't go well, it's important to be accountable and not blame others."

"Kate and I broke up this week. I blamed it on her for not saying much and because when she was called on in class she said she liked some other guy."

"She liked someone else when she could've been with the star quarterback?"

"I don't think she really likes David. David is one of the slower boys in class. I think she just said that because she was embarrassed to say I was her boyfriend." I thought for a minute. "I guess I could've laughed this off, but I blamed her. Then I just stopped walking with her instead of trying to talk to her. It's hard to be accountable for my actions. It feels bad."

"When you're accountable, it helps make you a better person."

I wasn't sure I was ready to start being accountable, but what Gramps said made sense.

On Sunday we traveled to Waterford to play the other Waterford team, the Cheetahs, which to me sounded like "the cheaters." We got there and did the weigh-in.

"120 pounds," said the official. "This boy barely makes it, but he can play."

I was so excited to play quarterback that I'd forgotten to watch my diet. Luckily, I was cleared to play.

The Cheetahs got the ball first, and they got a couple first downs but hadn't made it to midfield yet. It was third down and 8 yards to go, and I got ready to sack the quarterback if he tried to pass. I burst through the line as the quarterback dropped back to pass. He faked the ball to the back, and it fell out of his hands. I picked up the ball on the run, without having to break stride, and took off for the end zone. As I got closer, I could hear some players chasing me, but I was determined to make it. One player jumped on my back at the 5 yard line, but I kept going and dragged him into the end zone with me. I'd scored my first touchdown, and it was from the defensive end. I'd had an opportunity, and I'd made the most of it.

I gathered the team together for the extra point and decided I was going to run the quarterback sneak on the quick count and let them try to tackle me again. We took them by surprise, and I was able to get in the end zone before they could touch me. We led 8-0. I'd scored a touchdown and an extra point, and we hadn't even gotten the ball yet!

The next time the Cheetahs got the ball, they were able to drive down the field and score. They added the extra point to tie us. I finally got to go on offense in the second quarter. I mixed up the play calling quite a bit, and we were able to move the ball. We got down to the Cheetah 30 yard line, and I decided to try the reverse for the first time. I gave the ball to Stan but kept running like I had the ball. A couple guys even tried to tackle me. As I was carrying out the fake, I looked over and saw

Stan running into the end zone for the score.

For the extra point, I decided it was someone else's turn to get a score, so I called the tight end quickie. I looked left, saw Walt open and gave him the ball for a 16-8 lead.

We got the ball to start the second half. We moved the ball pretty well, but had a fourth down and 4 on the Cheetah 39 yard line. I knew this wouldn't work in college or pro football, but our best chance to get the first down was to run the quarterback sneak and not let them get me down until I had run far enough for the first down and Sure enough, it worked.

We kept the drive going and ended up scoring from 10 yards out on the option pass to Stan. For the extra point, I tried the quickie again and got the ball to the other tight end for a 24-8 lead.

Waterford got the ball again and drove about 50 yards before they fumbled again, and one of our linebackers was able to fall on the fumble. It was time for the second-team offense to come out, so I went to the sideline. My former group, now quarterbacked by Kevin, ran four plays and gave the ball back to the Cheetahs. The Cheetahs drove down and scored with only a minute left in the game, which made the score 24-16.

I went over to the sidelines for the kickoff, and Coach Patterson called me over.

"Tom, I want you to run the clock out and run all quarterback sneaks. Don't get fancy. Just hang on to the ball."

I went in and did what the coach had asked. Even though the Cheetahs were calling timeouts, I made a first down on the fourth straight quarterback sneak, and the time expired. We'd won our first game! Everyone was jumping around, and I decided it was time for me to celebrate too. Even I jumped around a little.

It was great to come off the field with a win. And I was happy that I'd played such an important role. However, I started thinking about it and if it wasn't for the fumble near the beginning of the game, it might have been a tie game. My thoughts then turned to next week. Would I get to quarterback the first-team offense again? Was Kevin ready to take the job back?

"Get back, get back,
Get back to where you once belonged.
Get back, get back,
Get back to where you once belonged."
— The Beatles (1969)

Get Out

The next week at school went well. I didn't brag with Steve in history class. I knew the Blue Devils had lost, and I'm sure he knew we'd won. I could've retaliated for his comments to me, but I didn't. I remembered that Steve was going to be my teammate next year.

Kate and I just went about our week like we didn't even know each other. I tried to accept her as being her. We really didn't hit it off that well. I figured I would someday regret the decision to walk away from one of the prettiest girls in the school, but I just thought there had to be more to a junior high school relationship.

Denny, Floyd and Stan did not share my thoughts on this at lunch that day.

"Man, you're skipping away from that foxy chick. Somebody forgot to oil The Machine," said Denny.

"Yeah, I'm hip, man. You need some of the Tin Man's oil," said Floyd.

"She didn't talk much," I tried to tell them.

"Sounds like the perfect girl to me. No talking and all kissing," said Denny.

"I'm hip," said Floyd, laughing.

"I don't worry about The Machine when it comes to girls. After Rocky and Kate, I can't wait to see who his next girlfriend will be," said Stan.

"Rocky?" said Floyd with a laugh.

"Roxanne, and is she foxy. Tom met her at the beach. Don't be fooled by the name. She is all woman."

In choir that week, we started learning a new barbershop quartet song called "Lil' Liza." It was a lot of fun. The baritones started us off with, *I had a dream the other night,* followed by the second tenors: *the sweetest dream of all.* Then my first tenors got to sing at a higher pitch, *I dreamt I saw your smiling face.* Finally the basses sang in really low voices, *beside the garden wall.* The refrain was sung in four parts and sounded really cool.

> *"Lil' Liz', I love you,*
> *Lil' Liz' I love you,*
> *love you in the spring and in the fall.*
> *Lil' Liz' I love you, Love you best of all."*

We really held that last note, and it sounded great. At home I practiced the song and, of course, I had fun singing all four parts of the verses.

On Friday, my mother told me she was going out with Vito. I decided to try to have a talk with her about him. "Mom, I appreciate everything you do for me. You make sure I get to all of my practices. You are there for me at all of my games."

"Thank you, Tom. I want the best for you."

"We need to talk about Vito."

"Okay."

"I know you like him, but I don't. He's rude to me. He can't say anything positive."

"Tom, he really likes you. That's just his sense of humor."

"Well, I don't like his sense of humor, and I want you to understand that I've had about all I can take of him."

"Tom, he's a good man."

"Mom, he's married. He's a cheater. He's a liar. I hear love is blind, but come on, Mom, open your eyes. I'm not going to put up with any more negative, smart-aleck comments from him."

"I'm really sorry you feel that way because he makes me happy."

"Well, would you do me a favor and tell him to lay off the negative comments and start apologizing for all his idiotic past behavior?"

"I really want the two of you to get along."

My mother didn't commit to talking to Vito, but I was happy that I'd been able to tell her what I was thinking.

Just then there was a knock at the door. I stared at my mother, and she looked back at me. She went to the door, and Vito came in the house. He tried to give my mother a hug but she backed up a little and turned and looked at me.

"Helen, I thought you had a son, but look at that hair. You have a daughter."

I sprang up from the couch and glared at Vito. The volume of my voice rose and I said, "What is wrong with you, idiot?"

"Why don't you control yourself? Why do you always embarrass your mother?" said Vito.

These comments didn't help the situation. The volume of my voice raised more. "Get out of this house, idiot! You're no longer welcome here."

"Well, your mother wants me here."

I looked at my mother, and I could tell she was starting to get upset. Vito had pushed me far enough. My voice raised to its maximum volume. "I SAID GET OUT OF HERE. ARE YOU THAT STUPID THAT YOU CANNOT UNDERSTAND ENGLISH?"

"Calm down," he said firmly.

"GET OUT, IDIOT! NOW! NOW!

He didn't budge. Then my mother spoke as she started to cry. "Vito, would you please leave before something worse happens?"

"Helen, Tom needs to learn that his behavior is inappropriate."

"YOU HEARD MY MOTHER, IDIOT! GET OUT NOW."

"Helen, you better do something about him, because if I leave I'm not coming back."

I wanted to keep firing at him, but I looked at my mother and waited for her to respond.

"Leave now," she told Vito.

He turned around, walked out and slammed the door as he left. She looked at me, crying, then went into her bedroom and shut the door.

I sat back down and watched television. I felt bad that my mother was hurting, but I thought I gave Vito what he deserved.

My mother didn't come out of bedroom to talk to me, so eventually I went to bed. The next day she got up and started making breakfast but still didn't say anything to me. I had breakfast and decided to go down to the lake and let my mother talk on the phone to whoever she wanted.

It was cold out that day, and I didn't see Gramps. I decided to sit on the log and think about what had happened. Did I overreact? Was this a ten on Gramps' one to ten scale? Was this like someone hitting me over the head with a baseball bat? The situation wasn't life threatening. If fact, it wasn't a threat at all. This was a situation where someone said something I didn't like. People at school don't call me a girl. Why did this adult have to call me this? I think what made the situation worse is that it happened inside my own home, where I'm supposed to feel safe. What also made it worse was that Vito hadn't said many positive things to me before, so this negative became magnified.

I'd also found out this guy was married. Was he ever going to really get divorced? Was my mother just a fling to him like she was to my father?

I finally decided the situation had been a five on the 1-to-10-point- scale, and Gramps had told me I shouldn't get angry unless it was at least a six. However, it happened, and it happened at home, so no one at school saw this—no teachers and no other students.

How did getting angry help me with my goals? It may have helped get rid of a guy I didn't like. He said he wasn't coming back. But my goals are to get along with people and not get angry, so I finally decided this didn't help me meet my goals.

My thoughts then turned to what to do now. I decided I needed to apologize to my mother and offer to do something really uncomfortable: apologize to Vito. As I headed back to my house, Gramps came outside.

"Aren't you cold?" he said.

"I'm good. I needed your log to do some thinking and let my mother have the house for a little while."

"Nothing better than a log near the water for some good thinking."

"Gramps, I had a situation with Vito last night, but I was able to think it through, and I've decided to apologize to my mother and Vito."

"You're one of the best thinkers I know. What do you think about the Spartans being able to beat Michigan today?"

"I think they can do it."

"I hope you're right. Do you want to watch the game with me? Ask your mother."

"I will."

I got back to the house, and my mother was on the phone. I sat and waited. With me back in the house, she stopped talking as much and then hung up.

"Mom, I didn't like being called a girl last night, but I've thought it over, and I want to apologize for my behavior. I've decided that if Vito wants to call me a girl and say other negative things to me, I'll try to put up with it. I'm willing to apologize to Vito as well."

My mother just sat and looked at me. "Tom, thank you. I actually thought about what you said about him being negative and being married. I was going to tell him last night that I wanted to end the relationship, but I didn't get a chance. You may not believe me, but I felt it was very mean of him to call you a girl. I wanted to trust that he would become more positive. I wanted to trust him that he was getting divorced. But my friends and my mother told me I was crazy. Love is blind. You are a smart young man. I really wanted to find love, and I didn't clearly see the entire picture."

"Mom, again, I'm really sorry."

"Tom, I'm proud of you. You've hardly gotten into any trouble. You've done so well on the football team. I hear all of the other parents saying what a good young man I have. I put you in a tough situation last night. I'm sorry for that."

"Mom, I'll try to do better the next time."

"There won't be a next time with Vito. You don't need to say anything to him. He's the adult. He should have acted better. A sense of humor is a good thing, but using it to hurt other people is not good."

"Mom, if you want to talk on the phone more today, Gramps invited me to watch the Michigan State game at his house."

"That will be fine."

I had fun watching the game. Both Charlie and Mollie and their families were there. Gramps' other daughter, Lucy, was not there because she now lives in Chicago. She was the only one in the family to attend the University of Michigan. All of Gramps other children (the ones at the house that day) had attended Michigan State and had on their green and white. It had been a rough year for the Spartans. They'd been shut out the last two weeks by Notre Dame and Ohio State.

"My team got shutout three weeks in a row but came back and won last week. Maybe the Spartans can do it too!" I said.

"The Spartans need you as their quarterback someday," said Charlie with a smile.

Mollie's son Todd, who was now 7 years old, wanted to play and not watch the game. I played with him about half the game and watched about half. Mrs. Davis had a lot of food, but I had to be careful not to eat too much since I had to make weight the next day. It was fun hanging out with

Gramps and his family, but the bad news of the day was Michigan beating our Spartans.

The next day, we had a home game against Milford. I got in line to get on the scale. "121 pounds. You have 20 minutes until you can weigh in again or number 11 won't be able to play today," said the referee.

I didn't go practice with the team. One of the assistant coaches took me and two other players to run back and forth. I was not happy about this. I didn't want to use all of my energy running. After about 20 minutes, the coach took us over to meet with the referee, and he weighed us again. I let the other two go first. The first boy made weight and Mark was ruled ineligible to play. Then it was my turn.

"120. Number 11 can play."

We ran back over to join the team. Mark took his helmet and shoulder pads off and put his jersey back on.

"Tom!" Coach Patterson called me over. "I'm glad you made weight, but you've used up a lot of energy. I want you to save your energy for quarterback. I am going to let Jeff start at defensive end. Rest up and get ready. I need you to lead the offense."

I did as my coach had requested. I didn't have a choice. *How good would our defense be without me?* As it turned out, I needed the time to transition from running and get myself ready for the game. Milford got one first down but then turned the ball over to us on downs.

I trotted out on the field with the team only needing 40 yards to go to get into the end zone. I ran a variety of plays and took the team down the field. We had a first and goal at the 6 yard line. I ran a sneak and got the ball to the 1 yard line.

Almost everyone on the team had scored except for our fullback, so I decided to run a dive play, give the ball to him and carry out the option fake. He got stopped at the line of scrimmage. But I decided to try the play one more time, and he made it into the end zone this time for the touchdown! We got the extra point on a tight end quickie to Walt.

We ended up winning the game 30-0. Being up by such a big score, my coach put the second-team offense in for our last possession. We were now 2 wins with 4 losses. The record was not stellar, but the win felt good. Milford had struggled in recent years, but next week's game would be against West Bloomfield, and we all knew they would be good.

Defensive End

"The Road is long,
With many a winding turn,
That leads us to who knows where.
Who knows where? But I'm strong!"
— Hollies (1969)

Weighing-In

The following Monday in history class, Steve didn't really congratulate me. All he had to say was that everyone beats Milford. He added that if we could beat West Bloomfield, he would be impressed. I got my test back in history and only got an 80. This woke me up a little. What was I doing? Just thinking about football and girls? I needed to get back to academics. I had committed myself to getting all As as my goal, but I wasn't getting an A in history.

At lunch, Floyd and Denny tried to draw up plays they thought I should run. They were coming up with double reverses, flea flickers, and streak passes.

"Tom, you gotta just send Stan on a streak down the middle. He'll outrun everyone and then you could throw the ball about 40 yards, and it would be an easy touchdown," Floyd explained.

I really didn't want them to know I could barely throw the ball 25 yards. If they knew, I probably wouldn't qualify as the quarterback for the school team next year.

"So are those the plays you guys run on the school team?" I asked.

They laughed. "You've got to be kidding. We run the blast almost every play. Coach Skinner believes in running the ball with two lead blockers. The only thing the defense doesn't know is if we're going right or left."

"You mean to tell me you're four and two and that's how you win?" said Stan. "I thought our offense was boring."

"Hey, but since The Machine can call his own plays, you should be passing about half the time," said Floyd.

I knew the guys were just joking around, but I felt they were criticizing my play calling. I just stopped talking. I wished I could come watch them play, but Denny and Floyd had their games on Tuesdays after school, when I was practicing.

On Thursday, Mr. Jett picked out four people in choir, one from each voice group, to perform "Lil' Liza" and "The Man on the Flying Trapeze" in the lunchroom the following week. Floyd was selected as the bass, but I was not selected as the first tenor. At first I was very disappointed, but then I started to think about it. *Am I really ready to perform a solo in the lunch room?* I was great at singing with no one home, and I blended in well in a choir. This would've been a great honor, but it would be terrifying to sing solo in front of the school.

Instead Mike was selected as the first tenor. He usually sings the loudest, and I try to blend in with him. I may have developed into a leader on the football field, but I was still a follower in choir. Mr. Jett selecting Mike helped me realize that if I wanted to keep going in singing, I had to get better.

On Sunday, we traveled over to West Bloomfield, which was actually closer to my house than the Walled Lake Western field where we played our home games. I'd been working really hard and watching everything I ate to make weight. I'm sure I was the only active 12-year-old boy who had to watch his weight. I didn't really have much fat on me, but I was growing taller.

"121. Number 11 can try again in 20 minutes."

My head sank. This weighing-in was ruining the fun of football for me. I went and ran, trying to shed the pound. After 20 minutes, I felt like I'd already played a full game. I went back over to get weighed again.

"120. Number 11 can play."

I could play, but I felt defeated. I went over to the bench and checked in with the coach.

"Tom, we have the ball first, but you look exhausted. I'm going to play Kevin for the first set of plays. Rest up."

I felt like I'd lost my starting quarterback job. I sat down on the bench and quickly worked to change my attitude. With Kevin at quarterback, we ran four plays and couldn't get the first down. Coach hadn't said anything about defense, so I went in to play with the first-team defense as usual. The other team's first three plays were runs up the middle, and they already had a first down.

On their next play, they ran the option my way. I tried to hit the quarterback just as he was pitching the ball to the tailback. When I saw this, I reached out my right hand and deflected the ball. Stan came running through, picked up the ball and ran full speed to the end zone. No one got a hand on him.

I started coming off the field, but the coach said, "Get in there at quarterback. Run the tight end quickie. Kevin, you're out."

I told everyone the play in the huddle and got up to the line and ran it. Walt looked open, so I got him the ball, and we had an 8-0 lead. The quickie was a short easy pass but since I was taller than Kevin it was easier for me to get the ball over the lineman.

West Bloomfield got the ball back on the ensuing kickoff. They combined running with passing and marched the length of the field to tie the game at 8.

The second team offense were on the field for the next four plays, and they were unable to get a first down, so I came back on the field to play defensive end. We were not able to stop the West Bloomfield offense again and were now down 16-8. I ran a few good plays, but we gave the ball back to West Bloomfield, and they scored again, making it 22-8 at the half.

We had to kick off to them to start the second half. On second down and 6, they tried a pass play, but I sacked the quarterback for a loss of 10 yards. Two plays later, we had the ball back.

I ran a few quarterback sneaks and some option plays, keeping the ball myself. I was determined to get the ball in the end zone. On first down and 10 at the 12 yard line, I called the crossbuck pass and hit Stan for a touchdown. We again tried the tight end quickie for the extra point, but both tight ends were covered, so I ran the ball toward the goal line and probably carried three opponent players with me into the end zone. It was 22-16. West Bloomfield scored again to make it 30-16, but we were not able to score another touchdown.

After congratulating the other team, I walked off the field with my head down. I'd tried but failed. I heard my mother call my name. As I looked up, I saw Gramps, who had come to one of my games for the first time.

"Good game, Tom," he said.

I looked up at him and said, "Thanks, Gramps." It really meant a lot to me that he'd come out to a game.

I kept walking, and then I heard a girl's voice. "Hey, stud quarterback. You're looking good. You need me as your receiver. Love the hair." It was Rocky.

I looked over and smiled. "Thanks for coming out. See you next summer on the beach."

"I'll be there. I want to get your autograph."

I smiled and shook my head. She had remembered what team Stan and I played on. She must have made some effort to look up the schedule. I thought about her instead of the game going home. As far as I knew, she'd only talked to those older guys for a half hour. I probably assumed too much. *Maybe I'll be closer to her height next summer.* I smiled with the thought.

On Friday, Mike, Floyd and the selected second tenor and baritone performed the barbershop quartet songs in the lunchroom. I couldn't believe how good they sounded. I also couldn't believe that they were able to sing and nothing bothered or distracted them. They just sang away like I did when I was home alone.

Could I have sung like that with all of the distractions and all of these students staring at me? Would I have been comfortable singing the high part in front of the girls in the school? Maybe they would have made fun of me. They all know my speaking voice is higher than many other boys is, but it doesn't stand out like it would singing. Someday I want to be comfortable singing the high part in front of everyone. Robert Plant of Led Zeppelin doesn't have any problem singing in front of thousands, and people don't make fun of him.

There was one thing more painful than the dentist: getting my hair cut. Every time I got my hair cut, the lady didn't do it the way I wanted, and I ended up really angry about it. Sitting in the chair watching her mess up was a painful process.

My hair was really looking good, but it was starting to get in my eyes and bother me. When I was playing football, I could put the helmet on so it held it all on my forehead. Maybe if I got my hair cut I could lose a pound for the weigh-in. This was long overdue, and my mother really wanted me to get it cut.

I drove with my mother to Pontiac Mall on Saturday morning. The agreement was that we would get Arby's for lunch after the hair cut. I didn't have someone who regularly cuts my hair. I just got whoever was available. The lady I got was overweight, not very good looking, and loud. I really didn't like loud people cutting my hair.

"Well, what're we going to do today?" she asked loudly.

"A regular man's haircut," my mother said.

"Mom, don't say that. She doesn't know you're joking," I snapped.

"Well, what da ya want?" she said loudly in her nasal voice.

"I just want it trimmed up a little."

"When was your last hair cut?"

"I don't remember."

"July!" my mother responded.

"Okay, let's see what we can do."

She started cutting, and it was going quickly—so quickly that I started to question her ability to cut hair.

"Wow, what are you doing?"

"I'm cutting the back. Most guys want the feathered look. Is that what you want?"

Her voice was giving me a headache.

"I don't know."

"Well if you don't know, how am I supposed to know?"

I decided it was best to just sit there and be quiet.

She finished up and brought me a mirror. "Well, what do you think?"

All I could think was that it looked different. I could see a lot of my hair gone, and I was stuck with it. I didn't say anything.

My mother paid, and we left.

"Tom, it looks a lot better."

"It looks horrible." I really did hate it.

"It will grow back."

I turned and glared at my mother. The only saving grace was the trip to Arby's.

On Sunday, we traveled to play Livonia. I wondered if Teresa would be there, but I never saw her. I'm glad she wasn't because at weigh-in, I weighed 123 pounds, and they wouldn't give me a chance to try to lose 3 pounds in 20 minutes. I walked over and signaled for my mother as I was taking my shoulder pads off.

"Tom! What is it?"

"I was three pounds over the weight limit, and they won't let me play. Would you please put my shoulder pads and helmet in the car?"

"Oh, Tom, I'm so sorry."

My mother took my equipment to car. I then went out to watch the warm ups. Kevin saw me, and he must have known he had an opportunity to show what he could do today. I yelled, "Come on, Kevin! You can do it today! We need you!"

After Stan ran out, he came over to me. "The Machine. Hey, man, we'll get this one for you. No Ding Dongs for you this week. I'm going to keep all food from you myself because we need you for the Blue Devils next week."

I really felt bad but took a break from my grieving to say, "The Man. You better get them today, or you won't deserve any Ding Dongs either."

I looked up into the bleachers to see if I could find my mother. When I saw her, she looked sad. I knew she felt bad for me having to sit out. I wanted her do feel better, so I got up off the bench and started encouraging my teammates.

The bad thing was that not only wasn't I the quarterback today, I had to be substituted at defensive end as well. The other team got the ball first and marched down the field. My replacement at defensive end wasn't doing so well.

On the opponent's first offensive possession of the first half, they ran the first three plays right at the defensive end, where I would've been playing. On all three plays, they double-teamed

Stan. They gained 31 yards on the first play, 8 on the second and 24 yards and a touchdown on their third. They'd found a weakness. I hoped the Blue Devils were scouting the game and would try the same approach next week, because I planned to be back. I figured if I made weight next week, I would get my starting defensive end job back, but I wondered about quarterback. Kevin was playing well.

I did my best to cheer on the team, but inside I just kept feeling how disappointed I was. We ended up losing 28-6. To make matters worse, the announcer said over the loud speaker that the Detroit Lions had lost to the Minnesota Vikings. The Vikings were the one team I really wanted the Lions to beat. At least I wouldn't have Vito coming around to rub it in.

After the game, I walked back, and my mother was waiting for me. She was so supportive. She didn't scold me about eating too much, and she didn't say she was going to put me on a diet this week. She was being Mom and waited to see what I wanted to do.

I went home wondering if my youth football career was over. How was I going to lose 3 pounds in a week? I had looked forward to playing the Blue Devils all season. Today was a big setback, but next week would be even worse if I couldn't play.

After I'd been home about an hour, the phone rang, and my mother answered. She mainly just listened and kept saying "yes." Then she said her goodbyes and hung up. She turned to me and said, "That was Joy Patterson, your coach's wife. Coach Patterson really wants you to play next week against the Blue Devils, but he understands that you're growing taller. Growing taller means you're putting on weight. Do you want to play next week?"

"Of course I do. I really want to beat the Blue Devils. What do I have to do?"

"Are you willing to eat a lot less this week and then not eat much on Sunday until after weigh-in?"

"Will this kill me?"

"No, but it's not ideal for a growing boy. This would be a big sacrifice you'd have to make to play next Sunday. Coach Patterson is going to bring a scale to every practice to see how you're doing."

"Mom, I'm willing to try it."

"Tom, I'm proud of you."

"Ain't no mountain high enough.
Ain't no valley low enough.
Ain't no river wide enough,
To keep me from you."
— *Diana Ross (1970)*

Rivalry Game

O n Monday after French class, Kay walked up to me. "I'm excited that we get to play against you this week. It will be a great game!"

"I hope so. I really want to play but I couldn't play yesterday because of the weight requirement."

"You don't look heavy at all."

"I'm tall. Height adds weight. My Red Devil career might be over. But I'll be there to cheer the guys on."

"We'll all be disappointed if we don't get to see the quarterback machine," said Kay, grinning from ear to ear.

In history, I talked to Steve, but he didn't look too happy. "Another Blue Devil win?" I asked.

"Tom, I didn't get to even play 'cause of this stupid weight restriction. My dad was really upset. He thinks they need to change the rules because boys grow throughout the season."

"I didn't play either. Same reason."

"Wow, I had no idea. All season we looked forward to playing each other. This would be a big disappointment."

"Hey, look, Steve, I don't want you to miss the game so you have an excuse when we win. No desserts. No pop. No second helpings. I want to see you in a helmet and shoulder pads."

Steve laughed. "I'll do my best. You guys can't beat us. We're four and four, and this win will get us to five and four. You guys have only won two games."

"You know what Woody Hayes and Bo Schembechler would say," I told him. "This is the rivalry game. Anything can happen."

At practice after school, Coach Patterson brought a scale.

"Men, this is a big week for us. We have the opportunity to finish as winners. But to win this game, we need our entire team. Joe, Mark, Sam and Tom, get up here. If these four guys play Sunday, can we win the game? We would have a better chance. I'm asking these four guys to sacrifice this week for the good of the team. Joe, get on the scale." Joe stepped up on the scale. "121, keep working. Mark?" Mark stepped up. "125. What have you been eating?" Sam stepped up. "123, keep working. Tom? 122 from our starting quarterback. We need you guys to lay off the sweets this week."

We repeated this ritual every day at practice that week. Kevin ran a lot of plays with the first-team offense in the case I couldn't play. It was a very hard week for me. I felt hungry, and I also missed drinking pop. But I remembered that there was no quarterback controversy if I made weight. The coach had declared me the starting quarterback.

On Friday at practice we all got on the scales again. Joe and Sam were at 120 pounds. I was at 119. Mark was still at 125.

"It's not over. I need you guys to keep up the diets for two more days. I talked to the Blue Devils coach, and he agreed that the four of you and his five players in question can weigh-in an hour before the start of the game. If you make weight, you can then eat before the game. If you don't, you won't play. You're not going to diet and then run an hour before the game. Now, give me your McDonalds orders, so you can eat before the game."

I told him I wanted two quarter pounders with cheese with everything on them, large fries, and a large orange pop. The other players gave their orders as well.

On Saturday, I walked down and sat on the picnic table at Gramps' house, staring at the lake. I started to rehearse all of the plays in my mind. I was determined to play my best. I thought about what I would do in different yardage and down situations. When I exhausted all of the plays, I started thinking about how I was going to make tackles on defense. I thought about what Charlie had told me—that the difference between good and great is just a slight edge. After thinking for a while, I went back home.

On Sunday, my mother gave me a small cup of fruit for breakfast. I got dressed in my football gear, and we drove out to Walled Lake Western to weigh-in. Coach Paterson and the other players from both teams who were over the weight limit were there.

"Who's first?" said the referee.

I stepped up on the scale. "119."

Steve, the Blue Devil from history, looked at me and nodded.

I was so excited. I would play. I then started cheering the other guys. Joe and Sam made weight, but Mark was still at 125, so he would not play.

I then watched the Blue Devils get on the scales. Steve made weight, but one of the other five Blue Devils did not. With one player from each team not being eligible, it seemed like a fair game.

We then all ran to Coach Patterson's car to enjoy our McDonalds. Oh my. A meal never tasted so good. After we ate, we just relaxed for about a half hour and let our food digest. Then the other players arrived, and we cheered them on as they made weight. After that we ran out and warmed up.

After warm ups, the coach told us to line up by number in the end zone. As they called our name and number, we ran to midfield. When we all got to midfield, we went to our sidelines. Then the Blue Devils did the same thing. This was great, especially for the guys who might not get their names called during the game. I couldn't help but to think how bad it would be during this special moment if I tripped and fell with everyone watching.

We had to kick off to the Blue Devils first, so I started on defense. I made my first tackle of the day on the second play, but it was after they had enough for the first down. They gained four more first downs and had the ball on our 15 yard line for a third down with 5 yards to go. They ran the quarterback option my way, and I was able to tackle the quarterback for a 2-yard loss by going after him instead of waiting for him to come to me.

The Blue Devils didn't kick field goals or extra points either, so they had to go for it on fourth down and 7 to go. The quarterback dropped back to pass, and I came after him. He passed the ball just before I got there, but it was incomplete. I didn't get the sack, but I'd made him hurry his throw. We did exactly what Charlie had said: *bend but don't break*.

We got the ball on our own 17 yard line. I ran a couple crossbuck plays but was faced with a third down and six. We were too close to our own end zone to call a pass, so I ran a quarterback sneak and gained 7 yards for a first down. I next ran the option to right and pitched to our tailback for 6 yards. I came back with the reverse to Stan. He gained 22 yards before being pushed out of bounds. On first down, I gave it to the fullback on the dive, and he gained 5 yards.

It was now time to try my first pass because with second and 5, they might be looking for the run. I ran the crossbuck pass. The Blue Devils bit on the fakes, and Stan was wide open. I threw him the ball, and he turned on the speed to score a touchdown. For the extra point, I tried the tight end quickie, but both tight ends were covered, so I ran straight ahead but couldn't get into the end zone. The score was 6-0.

We kicked off to the Blue Devils again, and they started driving the ball down the field. When the second quarter started, they brought in their second-team offense, and we were able to stop them on downs. We then had to bring in our second-team offense. I cheered for Kevin, but he was unable to get a first down, and I was back on defense.

The Blue Devils mixed up the plays well. It was first down on our 30 yard line, and they faked the dive and threw a post pattern to their wingback, who caught the ball and went in to score. They had a running play for their extra point, and about four of us combined for the tackle, but their back had already crossed the goal line. The Blue Devils led 8-6.

I now had 3 minutes to get us a score, starting from our own 32 yard line. On first down, I ran the option and took it myself for 9 yards, but the clock was running. I next tried the crossbuck pass, but both Stan and Walt were covered, so I ran the ball again for 5 yards. I tried the option the other way and threw to our right tight end, but he dropped the ball. I then just ran the quarterback sneak up the middle for 12 yards, and Coach Patterson called time out.

"Tom, we have 44 yards to go and only 1 minute. We're going to have to throw on the next two downs to save time. Run the option pass and then the crossbuck pass and see where we get."

I got back to the huddle and did what my coach had asked. Stan was covered on the option pass, so I threw the ball to our tight end, and he gained 6 yards with the clock running. We ran the option pass, and I threw the ball to Stan, but it was out of his reach.

It was third down on the 38 yard line, and we had one play left with 8 seconds on the clock in the first half. I looked at Stan.

"Can you score on the reverse?"

"I'll score."

I ran the play making it look like the option as I handed off to Stan, but their defense was waiting for him and tackled him for a loss. We jogged to our end zone down 8-6 at the half.

In the second half we got the ball first at our own 35 yard line. I was determined to do what it took to score. I started out with the quarterback sneak. As I broke the line, I gave the linebacker a head fake and gained 15 yards before three guys could haul me down at midfield.

I ran the option on the next play and kept the ball myself for a gain of 5 yards. I then went to the crossbuck, and our tailback gained 5 yards for a first down. I went to the dive play, and our fullback gained 3 yards. I stayed with the same play, and he gained 3 more. I then went to the crossbuck, and our tailback gained 5 yards and a first down at the 29 yard line.

I went back to the fullback dive, and this time he was stopped with only a 1-yard gain. I ran the quarterback sneak again and gained 6 yards. Needing 3 yards for the first down, I ran the crossbuck to the tailback, and he gained 5 yards, moving the ball to the 17 yard line.

I didn't want to get fancy and lose yardage. They'd been waiting for the reverse at the end of the first half. I decided to go to the fullback again, and he gained 4 yards. I ran the same play again, and he gained one more yard. I decided to run the sneak and let them try to bring me down. I gained 5 yards, and we had a first down at the 7 yard line.

"No one is guarding me," said Stan. "They're all trying to stop the run."

"Okay, Stan. I'm going to run the crossbuck pass right, and if you're open, I'll throw you the ball. If not, I'm running it."

As I ran to the right, I could see Stan was open, so I threw him the ball for the touchdown. I decided to try the same play for the extra point, and again Stan was open, so I threw him the ball, and we got the two-point conversion. We now led 14-8, but there was a lot of time left.

As I came to the sideline, Coach Patterson said, "You had a great drive, but now it's time to play defense. We need you on the defensive end."

The Blue Devils got the ball and gained a couple first downs as the third quarter came to an end. They had to put their second-team offense in. We only allowed them 1 yard in their four plays, and I was in on two of the tackles.

We got the ball back, but it was Kevin's turn on offense. Our second-team offense picked up 9 yards, and it was fourth down and 1 yard to go. If I was in there, I would run the quarterback sneak and make them tackle me. Kevin ran the crossbuck to the tailback and picked up 2 yards.

The first-team offense started to run onto the field but the coach said, "Stay here. White offense stay on the field."

"We could put this game away," I told Coach Patterson.

"I know you could, Tom, but I'm rewarding the second team for getting the first down and letting them run more clock out. These kids have practiced all year too." Then he called for the first-team defense to all come over. "Rest up a little because I need you to play your hearts out and shut this team down when you get back on defense."

The coach's plan worked. The Blue Devils got the ball back with only 2:15 left on the clock. It was time for our defense.

They came out throwing the football. On first down they connected for a 12-yard gain. We knew they were probably going to pass, so we needed to go after the quarterback. Stan blitzed on the next play and sacked the quarterback for an 8-yard loss. We came after the quarterback again and made him hurry his throw for an incomplete pass. On the next play, the quarterback threw to Steve, who gained 16 yards, but they were still 2 yards short of the first down. It was fourth down and 2 yards to go with only 24 seconds left in the game. They still hadn't crossed midfield.

On the next play, they ran the ball up the middle for a first down. There were 14 seconds left in the game. I dug in, and as soon as the ball was snapped, I shot across the line and sacked the quarterback. They tried to get to the line to run one more play, but time expired. We had beaten the Blue Devils 14-8. We lined up and congratulated the opposing players.

As we came back to our sideline to celebrate the victory, there was an announcement from the press box.

"Lion fans, Tom Dempsey of the New Orleans Saints with his club foot just beat the Lions 19-17 with no time remaining with a record setting 63-yard field goal."

Wow! The Saints had only won one game all year, and the Lions were 5-2. What a disappointment. But we weren't going to let it stop the celebration.

As I walked out, I saw Coach Skinner of the junior high school team.

"Mochina! You looked good. We need a tough quarterback on the school team next year.

"You bet, Coach." Wow, I stopped to think about what I'd accomplished in only my first year at quarterback. Sure, I made a few throws, but I mainly did it on my play calling and my determination to not let anyone tackle me easily.

Next I saw Charlie and Gramps, who had come out to the game and waited to congratulate me. I then saw Stan's dad, who congratulated me as well.

I kept walking and found Grandma and Grandpa Mochina, along with my mother's cousin Rod, and I thanked them for coming all the way out here.

Lastly, I saw my mother. It had been rough on her since breaking up with Vito. I gave her a hug and said, "Thanks, Mom. Thanks for everything you do for me. Now I need one more thing. I need to go to Le Grande Garçon!"

"What is that?" she said, looking puzzled.

"That's what my French teacher calls the Big Boy. I'm still hungry, and I don't plan on dieting anymore."

My mother gladly took me to Big Boy and let me get whatever I wanted. I ordered a brawny lad with a big onion on it. Stan and I had planned that he would ask his family to go as well, and we met them there.

On the way home from Big Boy, I was so happy that so many adults in my life had come out to see me. But one person was missing: my father. Maybe he didn't know about the game, although I'd told him I was playing football when I saw him at the funeral. I guess he had his own life. He would get more opportunities, though because I planned on continuing to play football.

Defensive End

"What'll you do when you get lonely?
And nobody's waiting by your side?
You've been running and hiding much too long.
You know it's just your fooling pride."
— *Derek and the Dominos (1970)*

School Dance

On Monday, most people were still talking about the rivalry game. And if your game is being talked about, it's fun being the winning quarterback. The talk started in French class with the girls.

"Let's get the star quarterback's autograph," said Melanie.

"Write-ez your name, *s'il vous plait*," said Kay.

The French teacher heard this and told us how to ask for an autograph in French, but it seemed too complicated for anyone to try to repeat.

"So, *Monsieur* Thomas was the winning quarterback," the teacher added, trying to mix in some French.

I wasn't sure how to respond, so I just said, "It was a close game, but we won 14-8."

In history class the teacher asked, "So who won the big game that some of you like to talk about so much?"

No one said anything at first, so I said, "Steve caught a pass for a big gain."

"So who won?"

I looked at Steve and finally he said, "We really don't know because the referees made some bad calls."

"Bad calls? What bad calls? This is the first I heard about that."

"We had a timeout left, but the refs wouldn't let us use it. We could have stopped the clock and scored a touchdown to win."

"The bottom line is that the Red Devils won," I said.

I couldn't believe he would say that. Why couldn't he just congratulate me? I didn't know anything about any clock controversy. I wasn't very happy hearing this.

At lunch I got together with Stan, Floyd, and Denny. I told them what Steve had said.

"Steve's a crybaby. Skip him. He needs an excuse for how badly his team played," said Floyd in his deep voice.

"Those Blue Devils couldn't beat my choir boy!" said Denny, laughing. "Did you sing them some high notes and put them to sleep?"

"I did what any good quarterback would do. I got the ball to a fast runner and let him do the rest," I said looking at Stan.

"I think they were surprised at how well we played defensively," said Stan instead of telling how he had scored all 14 points in the victory.

In English class we were asked to write a story, so I wrote about the game. It was easy since I knew the story well. I titled it "The Winning Quarterback."

The next day we got our papers back, and I was expecting an A, but when I turned it over, I saw I'd gotten a C. How could I have gotten a C? There were a number of grammatical errors marked and some comments at the end:

Tom, this paper sounds like bragging and is a little farfetched. You're welcome to resubmit another paper, and I suggest you choose a topic other than football. Maybe you can include a few struggles versus triumphs.

I've often struggled writing papers because I couldn't think of what to write about. I finally thought I had a good topic. I stopped and talked to the teacher after class and asked her what I could write about. She wouldn't give me any ideas, so I asked if it would be okay to write about how I felt when I didn't make weight the week before. She told me that would be fine.

In choir that day we began rehearsing our Christmas songs: "A Virgin Most Holy" and "Masters in This Hall." Both songs were about the birth of Jesus. Today these songs couldn't be sung in schools because of their religious aspect, but back then no one questioned them. We just sang what we were told.

When I got home, I told my mother about the Christmas songs.

"Tom, it would be great if you could sing one of these songs as a solo for a church service. Would you do it?"

"That would be great," I said, thinking it would be fun to be center stage and ignoring how terrifying it would be to have all eyes on me. I just kept thinking: *if Floyd can do it, I can do it.*

The next day at lunch, Denny asked the rest of us if we'd gotten permission to stay at school Friday for the school dance. We all had.

"Great. I need a couple wingmen like The Man and The Machine." He looked at Floyd and said, "And, of course, The Voice!"

"It's more like we'll be Richie, Ralph and Potsie and be there with The Fonz," said Floyd, looking at Denny.

We all laughed, but the nicknames of The Voice and The Fonz stuck.

On Friday, we all agreed to meet up near the choir room for the dance. Denny and Floyd wanted to show Stan the inside of the room and joked that this would be the only time he'd see it. We walked together toward the cafeteria where they were holding the dance. We each paid our $2 admission fee.

It was dark in the cafeteria, and they had "Iron Man" by Black Sabbath playing loudly so we could hardly hear each other talk. We walked around and looked for people we knew. I think the other guys were all waiting for me to go up and start talking to girls. They didn't realize I was probably not much behind of them on the anxiety scale when it came to starting up conversations with girls I didn't know.

As we walked around, we realized that we hadn't gotten the memo that this dance would be mainly eighth graders. We didn't see many seventh graders at all, and the ones we did see weren't the athletes or the popular kids we were used to seeing. The seventh graders in attendance were mainly "burnouts" or "freaks." We figured they probably got together and smoked when they weren't at school.

Finally Floyd said, "Okay, Machine, let's see how it's done. Show us how to meet chicks."

"Hey, we don't jump right into production. We're still in the selection process. If you start talking to one girl, the other girls won't like it. You have to make the best selection. I'm looking for my choice. You guys tell me who you like." I tried to explain to Floyd but maybe I was just procrastinating.

The student council hosted the dance and had created a kissing booth. For $2, you could take a girl in the kissing booth and kiss her. Our goal was to find a girl and get her in the kissing booth.

I saw an eighth grader named Kathie. She was probably in the freak group, but I really liked her long blond hair and long legs. She wore hip-hugger jeans and a shirt that stopped about three inches from her belt. I couldn't take my eyes off that mid-section and her hour-class figure. She was a bit of a hippie, but there was something about those big hoop earrings I liked too. She was certainly going to be my selection, but I didn't tell the guys.

"I made my selection. I want that girl over there," Denny said as he pointed to a girl standing in a group of three friends.

"Yeah, and I'll take her friend—the shortest one," said Stan.

"Fine. I'll go with the chubby one," said Floyd. "Come on, Machine. Introduce us so we can go in the kissing booth."

Somehow it wasn't as hard for me to speak to girls if I was just introducing others. And I had to show the guys I had the courage. "Follow me."

"Hi. How's it going? I'm Tom, and these are my friends, Stan, Denny and Floyd."

"Yeah, we know who you guys are. You're the seventh-grade jocks. I'm Kim, and this is Jan and Deb."

We all said hi to each other and tried a little small talk about the music and school, and then Deb said, "What do you guys think about the kissing booth?"

"Oh, let's go," said Floyd in his low voice.

"Jan, Denny wants to try the kissing booth with you, and Kim, Stan told me he wants to go with you," I said.

The girls all liked the idea, and they went to stand in line. Floyd and Deb were first. They were only in there about five seconds. Denny was next with Jan, and they were in there about the same amount of time. I had no idea if Floyd or Denny had ever kissed a girl before. We didn't ever talk about it, but they had now, and they came out all smiles.

It was Stan's turn. Stan and I had been friends for more than 2 years, and as far as I knew, he hadn't had a girlfriend or attempted to kiss a girl. I could hardly believe he was doing this. Stan and Kim walked in. We waited and waited. It seemed like they were in there for minutes. Finally, a member of the student council had to tell them time was up. Stan came out holding Kim's hand, and I will never forget the look on his face. I could tell he was grateful to me for arranging it.

We told the girls it was nice meeting them and kept walking around.

"Okay, Machine, we all did it. Who's your selection?" said Denny.

"I've been eying Kathie."

"Ooooh my, a very fine chick! Do you think you can handle her?" said Floyd.

"Of course."

I was shaking a little, but I had to show the guys I could walk over and ask her to the kissing booth. "I'll be back."

"Hi, I'm Tom," I said as I approached her.

"Tom, the seventh-grade jock with wavy blond hair. Nice to meet you. I'm Kathie."

I decided to just come out with what was on my mind. "Do you want to go in the kissing booth?"

"Oh, Tom, you're so cute, but I can't. My boyfriend is in ninth grade, and he wouldn't be happy if I kissed you. Thank you for asking."

I said good-bye and walked back.

"What did she say?" asked Stan.

"Timing. She really wanted to kiss me, but she has a boyfriend in the ninth grade."

"This is starting to remind me of the Rocky story," said Stan.

"Just my luck."

"Tom, it took a lot of guts to walk over there. You're still my hero. Hey, can I borrow your two bucks? I want to go ask Kim after seeing how long she was in there with Stan," said Floyd.

We all started laughing, but Stan said, "No way. Kim is mine. Dream on."

The next day, I went down to the lake. It was cold, and the water was starting to freeze.

Gramps came out of the house. He was all bundled up with a hat, coat and gloves. "Tom, it's too cold to be out today. And I have to take my lovely wife shopping, so I don't have much time. I'm just still so proud of how well you played in the last game of the season."

"Thanks, Gramps. It's just so hard to believe. I went from never playing quarterback to throwing passes at trees to backup quarterback to starting quarterback to helping the team win against our rival."

"Tom, you never quit. You believe in yourself. You keep going when many people would give up. I'm still shocked you lost the weight to even play in the game."

"Oh, man. That was the hardest part. I was starving all week. I'm glad that's over."

"Next week is the Michigan–Ohio State game. Both teams are undefeated. Both beat Michigan State this year. This will be a big game. Do you want to watch it with me?"

"Sure."

"Why don't you come an hour early, before the others get here. I haven't had a chance to really check in with you in a while. Also, I know you're probably going out to your grandparents on Thanksgiving, but I'm taking my family down to the parade. Ask your mom if you can go to the parade with us. I could drop you off at your grandparents' house after the parade."

"Wow! That would be great. I'll check with her."

"You are on a road.
Must have a code that you can live by.
And so become yourself.
Because the past is just a goodbye."
— *Crosby, Stills, Nash and Young (1970)*

Basketball Tryouts

On Monday, I rode the bus to school, and as usual I sat with Stan.

"Hey. You ready for basketball tryouts today?

"I'm all set."

"Good. I hope we both make the seventh-grade school team."

I'd started playing basketball as a fifth grader in a league of 11- and 12-year-olds. Stan's father decided to coach, and he picked me as one of his players. I really had to learn the game that first year, and I ended up scoring two baskets in eight games. I did scramble for some rebounds, though. I wasn't afraid of setting picks and having players run into me to help the team. I put a basketball backboard and hoop on a tree in the backyard and practiced shooting a lot.

In the sixth grade, I played with Stan again and was coached by his father. I did much better that season. I averaged 4.5 points per game with a lot more playing time. I was one of the taller boys and had developed much better basketball skills. Basketball was a lot more fun last year than the previous year. I had confidence that I could play well, and I kept working hard.

At lunch, Denny and Floyd joined Stan and me like they usually did.

"Stan, or should I say Casanova, what's going on?" said Denny.

Stan was embarrassed.

"Yeah, we thought The Machine was the ladies' man, but now we know why they call you The Man," said Floyd.

"Hey, I did the same thing you guys did," responded Stan defensively.

"Only much longer," said Denny.

In English class, I got my paper back and had improved my grade to a B. I still struggled with writing, but I was determined to keep working on it. Who knows? Maybe someday I could write a book.

In choir, we continued to work on the Christmas music. I thought my voice sounded pretty good on "A Virgin Most Holy," so I decided to tell my mother I would sing that song for the church. The first tenors had the melody for this song, and it flowed smoothly. The basses sounded like they were singing the same note throughout the song. Their part sounded funny alone.

On Thursday, Stan and I checked the list to see who made the basketball team. We were happy to see we'd both made the team. However, we went to practice after school and neither one of us was on the first team. The first team consisted of four guys from Union Lake Elementary, who had been to several basketball camps and had played a lot of basketball. Steve was one of the starters. The other starter was probably the tallest boy in the seventh grade, who already had facial hair due to being held back at least one grade. Stan probably made the team for his speed and athletic ability, and I probably made the team due to my height and hustle. Neither Denny nor Floyd had interest in trying out for the team.

On Saturday, I went over to Gramps' house to talk with him and watch the game. We went into a room Gramps calls his study, and he shut the door.

"Tom, this is the one room in the house that is mine. The only other room that's truly mine is the boat house. Now, first we have to test if the room is private. This isn't like sitting outside on the picnic table. We can do this by me telling you a housewife joke."

"Okay." I laughed before he even told it.

"The TV repairman came into a house and noticed the housewife was very attractive. When he got done fixing the TV, the housewife asked if she could ask him for a favor but not to tell her husband. She said she was a woman, and the TV repairman was a young man. Her husband was getting old. The man said, 'Sure. Just name it.' The woman said, 'Great. I need your help moving this console TV to the other corner of the room.'"

I started laughing again.

"Tom, the room is private because if Ruth had heard that, she would be in here mad at me." He smiled. "How's junior high school going?"

"It's going well. I think the football season helped a lot. I'm getting pretty good grades. I just made the school seventh-grade basketball team, but it's going to be hard to get playing time."

"That's great to hear that you made the team!"

"I try to use what you've taught me for anger control. I still get angry sometimes, but when I do, I try to use the one-to-ten scale and decide afterward how I should have handled the situation. But most of the time I can use the scale to prevent me from getting angry. I still have goals of not getting angry and getting along well with people. If something bothers me, I try to keep in mind my goals."

"Seems like you're doing well with the anger control. How're you doing with worrying?"

"Well, after the funeral, the plane crash and the singers dying from drug overdoses, I was pretty worried about dying and thought a lot about how much I want to live. Lately, I haven't worried about it as much. I remembered you told me it's okay to be sad when someone dies, but it doesn't help to worry about death when we're not dying. Gramps, sometimes I think about you being 50 years older than me, and it helps me to know I have a long life to live."

"Worrying is one of the most unproductive things people do, but so many people do it. So can you talk to beautiful girls now?"

"It's still tough for me, but I had one of the prettiest girls in the school as my girlfriend for about a month. I probably overreacted to one of her statements in class, but I realized we didn't have good communication, so it was hard to repair my overreaction."

"Oh, yes, I remember you talking about her. She didn't talk much."

"She was really good looking, but she wasn't that much fun. The only good thing that came out of it was the other guys thinking I could have that good looking of a girlfriend. Also, at the school dance recently, I approached a good-looking eighth grader."

"How did it go?"

"As it turns out, she had a boyfriend, but I did realize that getting turned down isn't as bad as getting beaten by a baseball bat."

"You gathered information. By approaching her, you found out whether she was interested or not. She may have been interested but now you know."

"The interesting thing is that she didn't say anything really bad to me. I think she may have liked me if she didn't have a boyfriend."

"I don't know why she wouldn't," Gramps said with a smile. "So, we had talked about defensiveness some. How is that going?"

"I think this is still hard for me. If someone says something wrong, I feel like sticking up for myself."

"You're right. It is hard. We learn at an early age to defend ourselves to avoid punishment. Criminals come up with some made-up stories so they can avoid jail time. But for you, you don't have to worry about jail time."

"I almost ended up in jail."

"I know that was a tough situation for you, but in a way, you got some good first-hand information about how criminals are treated. What did we talk about instead of using defensiveness?"

"You told me to understand, accept and appreciate. It's hard to do when I think someone is wrong."

"It really takes some work. It starts with understanding that defensiveness only digs us into a hole deeper and then setting a goal to try to express ourselves honestly."

"Sometimes it's hard to see that defending myself is not being honest."

"If you want to improve on being less defensive, I recommend setting a goal to be honest and to understand what people in authority or people you care about are saying, even if you don't agree with them."

"These sound like a good goals. Give me an example."

"Tom, that shirt is too loud."

I laughed. I hadn't heard of shirt being loud. "Loud?"

"Yes, it's so bright it makes my eyes hurt."

"I like it."

"So, Tom, you were honest about liking it, but I could've felt you were arguing with me instead of understanding. If you would've acknowledged that I thought the shirt was loud, you could have gathered further information. So if this was a teacher who said this, you could have said, 'I understand you think the shirt is loud. Do you want me to wear something different?' The teacher might have felt understood and then responded, 'No, wear whatever you want.' That comment might be good to hear because I know that's one of your favorite shirts."

"I'll set a goal to work on this."

"We also talked about being accountable and not blaming."

"Yes, this has taken some work. I tried being accountable for talking in class. I think I feel better when I own up to what I've done. Admitting to talking in class is not going to get me jail time, and I won't be beaten. When I tried it, I think it made the situation easier, and the teacher didn't have to keep telling me."

"Blaming seems like it could be a good thing to help someone feel better, but if having relationships is your goal, it isn't. Blaming is the poison for relationships. When you lost the football games, did you blame the coaches and your teammates?"

"I did the first few games. I blamed the coach for not playing me more, but I didn't say anything to his face."

"So you thought about blaming but didn't say it out loud."

"Right, but the coach could tell by looking at me that I was disappointed."

"I bet he could. I think he expected you to want to play and to be disappointed when you didn't. If you would've blamed him, it probably wouldn't have helped you eventually become the starting quarterback." Gramps paused for a moment and then added, "Tom, I've got one more thing I want you to think about. Do you ever think you know what others are thinking?"

"Yes. I do."

"This is called mind reading. We can think we know, but if we try to tell someone what they're thinking or feeling, it's easy for the other person to tell us we're wrong, because there's no way to really know. It's important that we only take what we're given."

"Take what we're given?"

"Yes, only use the information people tell us. People really don't like when you try to tell them what they're thinking or feeling. Even if you're right, they can still deny it. So try to keep in mind to only take what you're given."

"Gramps, I'll try it."

"I'm glad we got a chance to talk. It was just too cold to sit on the picnic table."

"Who are you going to cheer for in the Michigan–Ohio State game?"

"I'll just watch the game. I only cheer for Michigan State," Gramps explained. "You can cheer for whoever you want. Now, let's go watch it."

When we entered the family room with Gramps' color TV, Charlie and his family were there.

"Tom Mochina, the All-American quarterback and defensive end," said Charlie.

"Hey, Charlie."

"You won your rivalry game, and now this game between Michigan and Ohio State has become a rivalry. Michigan beat Ohio State last year in Ann Arbor after Woody Hayes and the Buckeyes had gone undefeated for three years. The fans in Columbus have gone nuts and declared this Beat Michigan week. The students at Ohio State have had rallies the last three nights. The fans will be loud."

"Who do you think will win?"

"Both teams are undefeated. Michigan beat Iowa last week 55-0. Ohio State barely got by Purdue 10-7. What bothers me is that the Ohio State fans now sing a song that they don't give a *bleep* about the whole state of Michigan. That includes us Michigan State fans, so how can we want the Buckeyes to win? It will be tough for Michigan to win in Columbus. I never thought I'd hear myself say this, but for today, *Go Blue!*"

As it turned out, Ohio State led at halftime 10-7 and went on to win 20-9. It was a lot of fun hanging out with Charlie because he was so knowledgeable about football, football history and the current players.

After the game, I went home, and my mother told me she was going out tonight. I would be home by myself. This was the first time I knew of that she'd planned to go out since the heated exchange with Vito. I listened and thought about my mother going out. Even though I'd had a bad experience in the past, I should try to give this new guy, Bob, a chance. Maybe he'd be a decent guy. He wouldn't be Charlie. Charlie had become my dream father, but he was married to a very nice lady so it couldn't ever happen.

When I met Bob, he was different than a guy I thought my mother would pick. He had a little longer hair and mustache. He wore bell bottoms and a mod shirt. He didn't say anything negative and acted like a hippie. I didn't talk to him long, so I didn't get to find out any more about him. I'm sure my mother was nervous about me meeting him.

"So I got me a pen and a paper,
And I made up my own little sign.
I said thank you Lord for thinkin' 'bout me.
I'm alive and doin' fine."
— *The Five Man Electrical Band (1970)*

Giving Thanks

I woke up Monday morning and remembered I had set a goal to take accountability for my actions, to gather information from others and to not be defensive. Being that this was Thanksgiving week, I only had three days of school to practice.

History class started with Steve claiming he was an Ohio State fan and had known Ohio State would win. I challenged him with a few of the facts Charlie had told me about the games the previous weeks, but just then the teacher said, "Tom, it's time to start class."

"Yes, ma'am. I'm sorry I was I talking. I'm ready."

"My name is Mrs. Behm, not ma'am."

"Yes, Mrs. Behm, I'm ready for class."

I tried to avoid calling her by name since earlier in the year people had joked that her husband was the guy who made bourbon, even though her name was spelled differently. Thinking about this sometimes made me giggle, and I did not want to giggle.

Did I meet my goals in this class? I took accountability for my actions by admitting I was talking. I gathered information that she wanted to start class. I took what I was given when she said she wanted me to call her by name, and I did. I didn't read anything else into it. I didn't think she was trying to disrespect me or make fun of me. I accepted her authority and appreciated that a teacher would want to teach and not hear an argument over a football game. Wow, this was a lot of thinking. I hope this comes naturally at some point.

At basketball practice, the coach called most of the players by their last names, but since Stan and I had such a long last names, he called us by our first names. We were running some drills, and all of a sudden the coach stopped us.

"Tom, do you really think you're going to score any points taking the ball up soft like that?"

I looked at the coach. I was just trying to put the ball in the basket. I didn't know how to respond. *Yes* would not come off well. *No* was not the truth. I just said, "Show me, Coach."

"Give me the ball! When you go up for a layup, you don't stroll up there like you're going to your grandmother's house. You go hard to the basket, jump as high as you can so you don't get your shot blocked, and lay it softly off the backboard. Can you do that?"

"You bet," I said, because I thought that's what he wanted to hear, even though I wasn't sure.

"Here!" He passed me the ball. "Now go to hole like you mean it!"

I ran hard to basket and jumped high. I tried to put the ball softly off the backboard, but it missed the basket.

"Much better. Now keep your eye on the backboard, and put the ball in the hole."

Later as we scrimmaged against the first team, the coach stopped our play.

"Tom, Tom, Tom, you call that a pick? Do you think you bothered the defensive player at all?"

"I   tried."

"Tried! Well, try harder! My wife tries harder than that." The coach demonstrated how he wanted the pick set. "You have to get right here to give your guard some room. After you've let the guy hit you, then you can roll to the basket. Got it?"

"Yes."

"Good. I come out here because I want you guys to be good basketball players. I could be home making out with my wife right now."

The next day, Stan was still laughing about practice. "Tom, you better give more effort than strolling to Grandma's because Coach could be home making out his wife. I couldn't believe you said you tried." He kept on laughing. Floyd and Denny got a good laugh out of it too.

I wish Coach had picked someone else for his teaching moment, but since it was me, I listened intently. I certainly would make every effort not to get singled out again. I wasn't the only player who caused him to stop practice, so when he stopped and coached someone else, I listened so I wouldn't make the same mistake.

On Thursday morning I went down to Gramps' house early to go to the parade. I rode with Gramps, Mrs. Davis and Lucy, Gramps' daughter who lived in Chicago and was home for the Thanksgiving holiday. Charlie and his family, as well as Mollie, Gramps' oldest daughter, and her family drove separately.

"So, Tom, you've never been to the Hudson's Parade?" asked Lucy.

"No. I've seen it on TV." I couldn't help but notice how good looking Lucy was.

"Oh my. I've been to so many parades. I'm glad you're bundled up because it will be so cold. I wonder if Santa will show up this year. Dad always wants to get there early to get by the J. L. Hudson building to see—"

"Now, Lucy, this is the prime spot to see the celebrities. We have a new mayor this year, so it will be our first time to see Mayor Roman Gribbs," said Gramps.

"It just won't be the same without seeing Mayor Cavanaugh," said Lucy with a smile.

"Also, we'll get to see the new Miss America, Phyllis George."

"I knew my dad would know Miss America's name. Now Dad, who do you really like to see in front of the Hudson building?"

"I can't think of anyone else, Lucy."

Lucy laughed. "We'll see."

"Ray, just admit it. Lucy knows. You want to see Christmas Carol!" added Mrs. Davis.

We got there and saved places for Mollie's and Charlie's families. It was really cold, but I enjoyed getting to see the bands and floats. The Hudson's parade didn't have the large character balloons like the Macy's parade in New York. I really felt special being included in this family. Todd, Mollie's oldest son, wanted to sit next to me the entire time.

Charlie provided the history comments. "What makes this parade different than all others is the use of these papier mache heads, which have been part of the tradition since before we started coming. If you look carefully, you can see they have a screen opening in the neck to let the person inside breathe and see."

After the parade, Gramps dropped me off at my grandparents' house. My mother was already there. "Did you freeze?" she asked.

"It was cold, but we got to see the new mayor and Miss America."

"Tom, I brought you some clothes to wear. Would you please change?"

Of course she didn't bring what I would have preferred to wear, but I changed. I felt a little funny when Rod got there. He was dressed much more mod, but I didn't have a lot of choices.

"Hey, how's the band going?" I asked.

"We haven't had a lot of time to practice, but now that we have four days off school, we plan to practice a lot. We want to try to play "Satisfaction" by the Stones."

I enjoyed talking to Rod, but Grandpa Mochina was more interested in the Lions game, so we came in and joined him.

"I like tradition, and we've always played an NFC team on Thanksgiving. For the first time ever, we're playing an AFC team, the Oakland Raiders, on Thanksgiving."

"How's the game going?"

"Not very well. It is almost halftime and the score is tied at fourteen. We can't seem to guard this white kid out of Erie, Pennsylvania, Fred Biletnikoff. He's scored two touchdowns."

"Are you ready to eat?" I heard Grandma Mochina ask.

"Just about. Sixteen more seconds until halftime," responded Grandpa.

"I know that means five minutes. Wash up, everyone."

I washed my hands and came to the table. I noticed Grandma had given me a plastic cup. Although I felt I was ready for glass, I appreciated her remembering what I'd asked for last time.

Just as everyone sat down, Grandpa Mochina asked everyone to go around the table, starting with Grandma, and tell what they were thankful for this year. It was interesting to hear what everyone said. Grandma was thankful for the health of her family, the happiness of her family, being in America and Grandpa's job.

It was my mother's turn next. She started with how thankful she was for me and how well I was doing in school, with my friends and in sports. She was then thankful for her job and all of her friends and family.

It was now my turn. What should I say? "I am thankful that I got to go to the parade today. I am thankful for the opportunities I've been given in sports. Stan's dad gave me an opportunity in baseball. Coach Patterson gave me an opportunity to learn the quarterback position. Now my basketball coach has given me an opportunity to learn basketball, even though I have a lot to learn about that game." I looked at my mother. "I'm very thankful for my mother. She lets me try a lot of things, even though some of them— like football— she thinks are crazy ideas. She puts up with me even when things don't go so well." I stopped, and Rod took his turn.

After a wonderful Thanksgiving dinner and pieces of both lemon and pumpkin pie for dessert,

I went back to watching the Lions game. The adults seemed to like the mince meat pie, but I didn't want anything to do with that. The Lions came back and won the so the entire Thanksgiving Day was a success.

"Tommy, can you hear me?
Can you feel me near you?
Tommy, can you see me?
Can I help to cheer you?
Oooo, Tommy, Tommy, Tommy, Tommy."
— The Who (1969)

Truthful End

O n Saturday, my mother told me she had another date with Bob. I tried to be supportive. I told my mother it would be okay to let me talk with him, so she agreed. When he arrived, I took the initiative to walk up to him and shake hands.

He seemed pleasant enough. This time he was wearing a peace sign around his neck.

"So what type of music do you like?" I asked.

He replied, "I really like folk music. I like the Mamas and the Papas, John Sebastian, Neil Young and Bob Dylan."

"Do you have any children?"

"Yes, I have one son who is now nineteen."

I wondered how old this guy was.

"So you like my mother?"

"Yeah, man. She's really cool."

My mother is cool? I wondered how long this guy would last. Bob and my mother went out and came back later.

—◆—

On Sunday we went to church, and my mother talked to the pastor, who agreed that I would sing "A Virgin Most Holy" the following Sunday. I was excited but very nervous about it. I had never sung a solo in front of a crowd of people before.

I went home and practiced the song many times. I thought I sounded pretty good, but wondered what it would be like to sing the song in front of a lot of people. I decided to walk down to the lake to see if Gramps was out.

Gramps was putting up his outdoor Christmas lights. When he saw me, he stopped and said, "So, Tom, what'd you think of Christmas Carol? Every year they come up with a Christmas Carol who's prettier than Miss America."

I smiled. "I agree that Christmas Carol was a babe. Do you need any help?" It was funny that Gramps wouldn't talk about Christmas Carol until he was alone with me.

"I almost have it all done, but I appreciate you asking."

"I get to sing a solo in church next week, and I'm nervous."

"Oh, no. You mean if someone doesn't like you, they might beat you with a baseball bat?"

"No. I know they won't beat me. But I've never sung in public before."

"You've sung the song many times in private though, right?"

"Yeah."

"So the only difference is your thoughts that other people are watching and judging you."

"That makes sense."

"What would be the worst thing that could happen during your performance?"

"Well, I could all of a sudden mess up, and everyone would laugh."

"Do you mess up in practice?"

"Never. I have the song down. Wait—once I cleared my throat in the middle of the song."

"So at this point, the song comes naturally to you and the likelihood of making a mistake is fairly small. However, you could make a mistake, and the people could laugh. Have the people at the church ever laughed at a soloist?"

"Hmm. I've never seen that happen.

"Me neither. I'm thinking that no matter how you sound, the congregation will be excited to see a young man up in front of the church singing God's word."

"Gramps, thanks for putting things into perspective. I feel much better already."

On Tuesday, we had our first basketball game against Milford. The game was a home game, and we played right after school. We played the first game, and then the eighth-grade team played right after us. The coach asked us to stay and watch the eighth-grade team rather than going home after our game.

As expected, neither Stan nor I started, and we didn't play in the first quarter. Our first team did well and got off to an 18-10 lead at the end of the first quarter. The coach called us together after the quarter had ended and told us who would play in the second quarter. He chose Stan and me and three other players. Even though my coach had scolded my efforts in practice, he still picked me to play on the second team. Since there were 13 players on the team, I was happy that I wasn't one of the three players to not be selected. There was a rule in junior high basketball that no player could play more than three quarters. This worked out nicely for Stan and me.

We ran the pick-and-roll play several times with me setting the pick and one of the guards driving by when their defender got picked. After a few times running this with the other guard, I had a chance to set a pick for Stan's man. I tried to get there and set a good pick so he could drive by and score. After I set the pick, I rolled to the basket. Stan made the decision to throw me the ball. When I got it, I went hard to the hoop, jumped as high as I could and hit the spot softly on the backboard to score the first two points of my seventh-grade career!

We ran the play several more times without success. Finally, when I picked Stan's man, Stan just drove as hard as he could to the basket and laid the ball up for the first two points of his seventh-grade basketball season as well.

We went on to win the game 49-33. The last two minutes, the coach put the other three players in the game since we had the lead. He also substituted Stan and the other second-team guard in to play the final two minutes.

After the game Stan said, "Tom, you passed the ball to me a lot this year in football. The least I could do is to pass the ball to you so you could score. I'm really glad that play worked."

Stan had become a really good friend. I knew he really valued our friendship too. Although he said he passed me the ball because I had passed it him, I knew he would have found a way to help me have a chance to score just because we were friends.

— ✦ —

On the day of my solo, we got to church early. The pastor asked me to sit up front, and as soon as the congregation finished "O Little Town of Bethlehem" I was to walk to the front, stand and sing my song. I told him I would do just that.

I sat down in the front row, and my heart started to beat more rapidly. I wished I hadn't volunteered for this. I turned around and saw Gramps and Mrs. Davis walk in to the sanctuary. I thought about what Gramps had told me. I have a singing talent, and people come to church to feel the presence of God. They weren't going to laugh at me. This was my chance to show people another talent I had. If seeing a 12-year-old boy sing a Christmas song helps one person go home and have a better day, it was worth it. If some think negatively about my performance, I will be fine. Of course, I'll probably never know it.

Just as "Oh Little Town of Bethlehem" ended, I confidently walked to the front of the church and turned around. I told myself, *just sing it the way you've practiced it*. I stared at the wall in the back. I opened my mouth and tried to get good tone as I started to sing,

> *"A virgin most holy,*
> *as the prophets did foretell,*
> *has brought forth a savior,*
> *our lord Emanuel."*

After getting this much out, I started to feel confident and then looked around at the

congregation. Some were looking at me. Some
were looking down. I went into the higher notes of

*"To be our redeemer from death
and from sin.
Christ Jesus, our savior,
has wrapped us in."*

    I finished, I looked down and started to
walk back to the front row. Most of the time when
my mother does a solo, she walks back in silence.
But I heard a few claps, and then the entire
congregation started clapping. As I sat down, I
smiled. People appreciated me. It was a relief that
it was over.

    The minister gave his sermon. Since I was
sitting in the front row, I didn't have much of a
choice but to listen. He talked about how the
holiday season should be about love and giving. He
asked the congregation if they wanted to be on the
truthful end or the defensive end. I perked up
hearing these terms. He gave examples of families
who are arguing or not talking. He said during the
holidays is a good time to communicate honestly
and not be defensive and blaming. He said playing
defensive end is good on the football field, but that
he wanted this holiday season to be about giving
and truthfulness.

    Near the end of the service, the minister
invited all to participate in the Lord's Supper. The
ushers passed a tray of little grape juices and bread
wafers to everyone. Each person had the option of
taking the juice and bread. I liked that he had
invited everyone to participate. At Vito's church, I
knew I would be excluded from participating since
I wasn't Catholic. I thought it best to accept the

practice of each church and not hold this against Catholics.

To conclude the service, the minister told everyone to go in peace. As I walked out I saw Gramps and Mrs. Davis who congratulated me for doing such a good job. I thanked them for coming to the service. Other people told me I did a good job as well.

Then my mother was there and told me how proud she was of me. I smiled and thanked her.

I looked up and saw an older lady. I expected she might also tell me I'd done well, but she said, "You looked a little shaky up there, son!"

My first thought was that she shouldn't be saying something negative. Then I thought she was an old woman and must have acted like she normally does. If she'd congratulated me, it might have been out of character for her. I wasn't wearing my coat of buttons and I wasn't going to take the defensive end after I'd just been inspired by the sermon.

"I understand I looked shaky to you. Thank you for your comment. Thank you for coming to the church today. I hope you have a merry Christmas."

She looked at me and didn't say anything. She might've been expecting a defensive response and didn't know what to say when she didn't get it. I still didn't really like her comment and wished she'd kept it to herself. I like to be around positive people, but I'm going to have to live my life with people who won't always act the way I want them to act. I am determined not to wear my coat of buttons and try to not be on the defensive end of communication.

References &
Recommended Readings

Ellis, Albert. 1975. *A Guide to Rational Living*.
    Chatsworth, CA: Wilshire Book Company.

Ellis, Albert. 1997. *How to Control Your Anger
    Before It Controls You*. New York:
    Kensington Publishing Corp.

Gottman, John M. 1999. *The Seven Principals for
    Making Marriage Work*. New York: Three
    Rivers Press.

Grant, Barry. 2010. Getting the Point: Empathic
    Understanding in Non-Directive Client-
    Centered Therapy. *Person Centered and
    Experiential Therapies*, 9, 220-235.

Tamm, James W. & Luyet, Ronald J, 2004.
    Radical Collaboration. New York:
 HarperBusiness.

Acknowledgments

Dan Bennett – Thank you for your review suggestions and being the first to catch my mistakes. Your experiences living in the area and playing football with the Blue Devils were very helpful.

Jacqueline Nguyen – Your insight is priceless in pointing out many things from the female perspective. Your ideas get me thinking and helped tremendously.

Jessica Royer Ocken– You are an extraordinary editor. I'm so glad I found you.

Jim Render – Your artwork of the stone wall is a great representation of what this book is about.

To everyone who has read this book – Thank you. It means a lot to me. I hope you enjoyed *The Baseball Bat*, The third book in this series, *Throw a Good Pass* will be coming soon.

To everyone who took the time to give me feedback or write a review publicly – Thank you. I value your feedback.

About the Author

James Shaw, PsyD, was born in Pontiac, Michigan, and lived in the metropolitan Detroit area through high school. He is now a licensed psychologist and clinical assistant professor at The Ohio State University Wexner Medical Center Family Practice.

27464093R00115

Made in the USA
Charleston, SC
12 March 2014